THE GREAT
AMERICAN
HOT DOG BOOK

THE GREAT AMERICAN HOT DOG BOOK

Recipes *and* Side Dishes *from* Across America

by Becky Mercuri

Gibbs Smith, Publisher
TO ENRICH AND INSPIRE HUMANKIND

Salt Lake City | Charleston | Santa Fe | Santa Barbara

This book is dedicated to my nephew, Robbie Mayerat, a truly gifted and creative chef who kindly endures his aunt's constant bragging and occasional interference.

First Edition
11 10 09 08 07   5 4 3 2 1

Text © 2007 Becky Mercuri
Photography © 2007 as noted at right

Published by
Gibbs Smith, Publisher
P.O. Box 667
Layton, Utah 84041

Orders: 1.800.748.5439
www.gibbs-smith.com
Designed by Douglas Dearden/Goodie Design
Printed and bound in Canada

Library of Congress Cataloging-in-Publication Data

Mercuri, Becky.
The great American hot dog book / by Becky Mercuri. — 1st ed.
   p. cm.
ISBN-13: 978-1-4236-0022-0
1. Frankfurters—United States. I. Title.

TX749.M447 2007
641.8'4—dc22

           2006020463

Photography Credits

Blackies, Hot Grill, Yocco's
www.roadfood.com

Blue Light, Curtis' Coney Island Famous Weiners, Original New York System, Rawley's, Rutt's Hutt, Tail O' The Pup, Wasses Hot Dogs
www.hollyeats.com

Gilley's PM Lunch
www.gilley'spmlunch.com

Nathan's Famous
Rob Kuchar

Papaya King
www.papayaking.com

Ted's Hot Dogs
www.tedsonline.com

Spike's Junk Yard Dogs
www.planet99.com

The Varsity
www.thevarsity.com

The Texas Tavern
Garneau Weld Photography,
www.garneauweld.com

Stewart's Original Hot Dogs
www.roadsidenut.com
Minnesota State Fair
www.minnesotastatefair.org

Skyline Chili
www.skylinechili.com

Iowa State Fair
www.iowasatefair.com

Tony Packo's
www.tonypackos.com

Walldrug
www.walldrug.com

James Coney Island
www.shutterfly.com

Pink's
www.pinkshollywood.com

Puka Dog
http://katiet.yelp.com

Good Dog Bad Dog
Molly Holzschlag
http://molly.com

Contents

Acknowledgments

When Gibbs Smith, president of Gibbs Smith, Publisher, asked if I could write a book on hot dogs, I wondered just how many different ways hot dogs could be served and if there was enough material for a cookbook. Little did I know! After agonizing for months over what great hot dogs to include and regretfully having to eliminate others, I know that Gibbs was right in proposing this book. I thank him for presenting me with such a fun opportunity. I am also endlessly grateful to Suzanne Taylor, vice president and editorial director of Gibbs Smith, Publisher, for her cheerful support and encouragement.

Any book delving into the history of food necessarily involves a huge amount of research. Unfortunately, it wasn't until recently that the history of food was thought worthy of recording, and when it came to hot dogs, available information was fraught with urban legends. Years of research were eliminated thanks to the kindness of word researchers Barry Popik and Professor Gerald Cohen of the University of Missouri-Rolla who so generously shared the fruits of their own labor as well as that of the late David Shulman. I am forever grateful to them, and to Barry, I send a special thank-you for quickly and patiently finding the answers to my endless questions.

A hearty thank-you goes to all the proprietors of hot dog businesses who took the time to share their stories with me; it is clear these folks love what they do. I'm indebted to numerous other people who assisted me along the way. John Fox is a frank fanatic who should be anointed "Dean of Dogs" for both his knowledge and willingness to assist in any quest for a fine frankfurter. The following individuals assisted me in ways too numerous to list: Bill Green, Philip Boas, Cary Boshamer, Dave and Jackie Brayden, Lavonne Riedel, Betty Brookshire, Joan Henry, Elyse Friedman, Rocky Hibbert, Ron Gardner, Rock McNelly, and Donna McDaniel.

As always, I thank my intrepid agent Meredith Bernstein. My editors, Jennifer Maughan and Melissa Barlow, are truly appreciated for their fine editorial guidance and for producing this book as envisioned so many months ago.

Special thanks go to Richard Boas and Tony Green who valiantly served as chief tasters during my testing of recipes for this book and who made many valuable suggestions along the way.

Finally, I must pay tribute to two websites that provided terrific leads for America's greatest hot dogs. Holly Moore's website at hollyeats.com serves as a compendium of many of the finest hot dog eateries in the United States. I'm not sure that Holly would appreciate being called the "Hun of Hots," but that's how I think of him. Jane and Michael Stern's site at www.roadfood.com was also an excellent resource for truly great hot dogs.

Introduction

Hot dogs are the essence of summer. For most folks, they're an integral part of a trip to the ballpark, where attendees consume about 24 million hot dogs annually. Hot dogs are one of our favorite comfort foods, evoking fond memories of childhood and fun times at picnics and family cookouts. Generally sold at mom-and-pop eateries, hot dogs also serve as a tasty alternative to typical fast food. Because they're so quick and easy to prepare, the hot dog is often served at home, especially by families with small children. America's hot dog consumption continues to rise, recently topping off at an annual figure of around 20 billion. In short, the hot dog is an American icon, loved by "kids" of all ages.

Many devotees of hot dogs enjoy traditional toppings like mustard and relish. Today, however, the humble hot dog has gone uptown and has become gourmet, dressed up in numerous creative toppings. A tour of America's finest hot dog stands, street carts, and restaurants tell the story of how the hot dog has evolved and become even more firmly entrenched in America's culinary traditions and food identity. Not all hot dogs are created equal, and specialties are found throughout the country. Different regions have their own favorite hot dogs. For example, New Yorkers are fond of hot dogs topped with sauerkraut and mustard, but to folks in the Midwest, Chicago-style dogs are the number one choice. Southerners love their slaw dogs, and chili is favored in the West. The Pacific Coast region favors veggie dogs and succulent old-world sausages.

In addition to delicious recipes for preparing great hot dogs and toppings, I've included instructions for some fabulous french fries that are natural accompaniments to hot dogs. Fries are often served with wonderful sauces like Mississippi's famous comeback sauce or Utah's fry sauce. You've got to try the Southern deep-fried pickles—yum!

As I researched and tested recipes, I was continually amazed by America's ingenuity, creativity, and proclivity for turning the humble hot dog into gloriously good eating. Sausage from the Old World was truly reinvented into a uniquely American food. I'm reminded of a conversation I had with Kamal Ali of Ben's Chili Bowl in Washington, D.C., when he observed that his parents, like so many other Americans, started a successful family-owned business based on hot dogs. Kamal had watched Rick Sebak's PBS special, *A Hot Dog Show*, and he noted that every story was similar and, "Almost any one of those stories could have been about my family." Second- and third-generation family members now run many of the hot dog eateries featured in this book, and everyone is tremendously proud of being a participant in such an all-American enterprise.

Don't be afraid to experiment. Mix and match sauces and toppings to come up with your own favorite combinations. I'm especially fond of Sahlen's beef-and-pork hot dogs, made in Buffalo, New York, topped with Rhode Island New York System Hot Wiener Sauce and Eastern North Carolina Coleslaw. With this book, you can fire up the grill and indulge in some truly tasty American hot dogs!

— Becky Mercuri

CHAPTER 1

The Real Story of the American Hot Dog: Debunking the Urban Legends

A great deal of the information presented in this chapter is based on the tireless efforts of the late David Shulman, Professor Gerald Cohen of the University of Missouri-Rolla, and New York City attorney, judge, and word researcher, Barry Popik. Their generosity in sharing the wealth of important information that they have gathered, in advance of their own landmark work on the origin of the term hot dog, *is greatly appreciated.*

Sausages date back to ancient Greek and Roman times. Bruce Kraig, hot dog scholar and Professor Emeritus at Roosevelt University in Chicago, says that it was the Austrians and Germans who specialized in sausages, tracing the first known references to "frankfurter wurst" to seventeenth-century Frankfurt, Germany. Vienna (Wien) sausage was known as wiener, leading to one of the terms used today for hot dogs. German immigrants brought sausages to the United States in the nineteenth century, and it's believed that pushcart vendors were selling them on the streets of New York by the 1860s. Sausage makers at that time would have made them based on recipes brought from the Old World. It wasn't until the turn of the twentieth century that hot dogs as we know them today made their appearance. The introduction of new machinery that finely ground the ingredients into an emulsion paved the way for the manufacture of the all-American hot dog. For many years, most people referred to the hot dog as a sausage or frankfurter, with the term *hot dog* eventually gaining favor.

Nikita Kruschev enjoying a hot dog while visiting the 1956 Kansas State Fair. Photo courtesy of the National Hot Dog and Sausage Council.

Coney Island Popularizes the Frankfurter

German immigrant Charles Feltman, said to have been a street vendor, has long been credited with being the first to sell frankfurters in Coney Island sometime around 1864. However, recently discovered articles in the *Brooklyn Eagle* archives indicate that Feltman didn't arrive in Coney Island until 1874, and it's noted that he was a baker seeking sales opportunities, not a street vendor. By 1875, Feltman had sold his bakery, and his elite Ocean Pavilion, a resort catering to the wealthy, was in operation, renowned for its seafood. An 1886 newspaper article mentions Feltman as one of several leading businessmen who decried the arrival of the common folk in Coney Island, brought by affordable railroad fares. Feltman also roundly condemned the "sausage stand nuisance," making it unlikely that he introduced the frankfurter to Coney Island.

Interestingly, the *Brooklyn Daily Times* of March 7, 1904, carried the obituary of Ignatz Fischmann, a longtime baker in Coney Island credited with creating the "oblong roll that the frankfurter men needed in their business." It's believed that the rolls, usually called milk buns, came into use sometime in the 1880s. The article goes on to cite Fischmann as "the inventor of the toothsome frankfurter sandwich that has helped to make Coney Island the most famous seaside resort on the Atlantic coast" and concluded, "Visitors to Coney Island did not feel as though they had 'done' the resort thoroughly without devouring a hot 'frankfurter and.'"

In 1916, Nathan Handwerker, a Polish emigrant, established Nathan's, the famous hot dog business that continues today. According to a newspaper interview with Handwerker in 1952, he visited Coney Island and saw a help-wanted sign at Feltman's, which he described as the most popular sausage purveyor in Coney Island at the turn of the century. (One might conclude that Feltman later had a change of heart when he realized the money to be made in selling frankfurters.) Handwerker applied for the job at Feltman's, and by saving the money he earned, he was soon able to open his own stand. Handwerker sold sausages at five cents each, half the price of the competition. He is credited as "the man who brought the hot dog to the people."

The popularity of the sausages sold at Coney Island attracted a great deal of attention, and it wasn't long before sausage vendors were found in many other locations and venues, including ballparks.

The True Origin of the Term "Hot Dog"

The tale has often been told that Thomas Aloysius "Tad" Dorgan, a sportswriter and cartoonist for the *New York Evening Journal*, was responsible for introducing the term *hot dog* to America. As the story goes, he was attending a New York Giants baseball game at the Polo Grounds in 1901. Sausage vendors, employed by food concessionaire Harry Stevens, were calling out, "Get your red hots! They're red hot!" and Dorgan was inspired to draw a cartoon depicting a dachshund in a roll. Because he supposedly couldn't spell dachshund, he captioned the cartoon with the term *hot dog* and established the marriage between baseball and hot dogs forever.

Despite the continued circulation of this story, among others, as one of America's most popular urban legends, it is simply not true. Researcher Leonard Zwilling conducted an exhaustive study of all the TAD cartoons and found no evidence of the legendary dachshund drawing. Professor Gerald Cohen points out that Dorgan wasn't even in New York in 1901, and the idea that a writer wouldn't know or at least look-up the spelling of the word dachshund is ludicrous. A 1906 TAD cartoon featuring a hot dog was discovered, but it related to a bicycle race, not baseball, and by that time, the term *hot dog* was already in use, albeit limited.

So where did the term *hot dog* originate? David Shulman had long believed that the answer was to be found in college slang, not Coney Island or the Polo Grounds, and Professor Gerald Cohen agreed. Enter Barry Popik, word origin sleuth extraordinaire. Popik doggedly pored over issues of the *Yale Record,* and he triumphantly found the elusive evidence in the October 19, 1895, issue in an article entitled "The Abduction of the Night Lunch Wagon," describing students who "contentedly munched hot dogs."

In those days, it was a common joke (and not always without some truth) that sausages were indeed made from dog meat. The students thus adopted the irreverent term *hot dog*, dubbed lunch wagons selling the sandwiches as "dog wagons," and referred to those partaking of the comestible as members of a "kennel club."

Although the term *hot dog* came into use in the 1890s, it continued to be negatively associated with dog meat. In 1913, the Coney Island Chamber of Commerce actually passed a resolution forbidding use of the term on signage. Even the hot dog itself was banned on occasion. An article in the *New York Times,* dated June 24, 1913, carried the headline, "Asbury Bans Hot Dogs" and recounted the fact that the mayor of Asbury Park, New Jersey, had taken steps to prevent a boardwalk vendor, Murphy & Krug, from openly selling their specialty on Sunday because such activity did ". . . not add to the dignity of the beach." Murphy & Krug were, however, given permission to sell hot dogs from the rear of the restaurant, but the vendor in open defiance publicly offered them for sale. A policeman was then posted at the front entrance of the restaurant and turned customers away.

On April 12, 1916, the *Los Angeles Times* published an article stating, ". . . the (Pomona) City Council today passed a resolution ordering Mrs. W. A. Blodgett, who handles the Ganesha park concessions, to refrain from displaying in her lunchroom or in any other place in the park signs referring to articles of food as 'hot dogs,' 'bow-wows,' 'ki-yis,' 'red hots' and other things suggestive of the most common variety of hash slinging." Nine years later, controversy still raged—a September 27, 1925, *Los Angeles Times* article stated, "The 'hot dog' is doomed by decree of meat packers. Not the dainty which has become almost the national food of tourists and pleasure seekers, but the name. The packers say the succulent sausage within a roll properly garnished with piccalilli and decorated with mustard, deserves a better name. Call them 'red hots,' or 'hots,' is the plea made in a nation-wide campaign."

The Rapid Spread of America's Hot Dog Industry

While debate swirled around use of the term *hot dog,* the humble little sausage actually spawned a major industry. Huge numbers of immigrants passed through New York City in the late nineteenth and early twentieth centuries, and many witnessed the success of the hot dog business in Coney Island. They seized upon a golden opportunity to earn a living in their new homeland. Although there is no evidence that Coney Island vendors sold their sausages enhanced with chili or a similar type sauce, many immigrant vendors devised sauce recipes that would differentiate their own hot dog businesses as they fanned out across the country. It has been speculated that some immigrant groups, notably the Greeks, formed networks and even provided a basic "Coney Island" sauce recipe to friends and associates seeking to establish hot dog eateries. Many of these entrepreneurs advertised their "Coney Island sauce" or named their businesses after the famous amusement park in Brooklyn.

On April 13, 1913, the *Atlanta Constitution* placed the ever-increasing popularity of the hot dog into perspective:

From the purlieus of the Great Boulevard of Blaze [a reference to New York's Broadway, also known as the Great White Way or the Lane of Light] *to the most isolated jerk-water hamlet in Mississippi, it has made the air fragrant with the seductive aroma of onions and sauerkraut, and has become an industry which is the means of separating the American people of millions every year.*

The early use of chili by Greek vendors is documented in this same article:

Atlanta's Greeks, the men who control the "hot dog" industry here, have old Julius Caesar and his compatriots skinned two ways from Sunday in the gentle art of lifting the coin. In five years gone by, they have made the Sherman act blush with shame. They are the compeers of every other nation when it comes to forking "hot dogs" and spreading the mustard, chile, and the sauerkraut.

Indeed, Greek immigrants were establishing hot dog businesses in numerous American cities and towns. By 1917, American Coney Island was operating in Detroit, Michigan, home to a significant Greek emigrant population. Empress Chili was founded in Cincinnati, Ohio, in 1922, launching the definitive Greek-style chili now called Cincinnati chili that is so popular in that region. In Alabama, another popular destination for Greek emigrants, Pete's Famous Hot Dogs was established in Birmingham in 1915, followed by Chris' Hot Dogs in Montgomery in 1917.

Throughout the United States, entrepreneurs who made a lasting contribution to American foodways and hot dog culture created an impressive array of specialty hot dogs. Their delicious legacy is still enjoyed today, as evidenced by a few examples here.

Jersey's Hot Texas Weiners

Following the success of the hot dog at Coney Island, it didn't take New Jersey boardwalk vendors long to follow suit and cash in on the popularity of the cheap snack so much in demand by bathers and promenaders. The hot dog was popular on the boardwalk by the early 1900s.

Soon thereafter, New Jersey's famous Hot Texas Weiner was born. Timothy Lloyd has researched and documented *Paterson's Hot Texas Weiner Tradition*, written in 1995 for the Library of Congress American Folklife Center. It's said that the Texas Weiner originated in the Paterson, New Jersey, area in 1924, and it's actually claimed to be the forerunner of the Coney Island hot dog served with sauce (versus the Nathan's original style Coney Island that's served with sauerkraut and mustard). The legend is interesting, stating "an old Greek gentleman" invented the sauce as he fiddled with various chili-type sauces to serve on hot dogs, thus differentiating his downtown Paterson stand from those operated by competitors. The man drew on his own culinary heritage, coming up with a sauce that is described as a kind of Greek spaghetti sauce, composed of tomatoes, ground meat, onion, and a secret mixture of spices that typically includes allspice, cayenne, cinnamon, and cumin. In the 2002 edition of *Roadfood,* Jane and Michael Stern cite information they obtained from hot dog historian Robert C. Gamer of Wyckoff, New Jersey. Gamer states that the first Texas Weiner stand was located in the Manhattan Hotel in Paterson before 1920, and the now-famous weiner with sauce was invented by John Patrelis, who worked at the stand owned by his father. Patrelis thought his sauce was similar to Texas chili, and in 1920 the name of the stand was changed to the Original Hot Texas Weiner. The incorrect spelling of the word *wiener* began then, and is still proudly misspelled today.

New York System Wieners

Rhode Island refers to its unique preparation of wieners as the "New York System." It's said that this term dates back to the 1920s when vendors, mostly Greek immigrants, arrived in Providence via New York and brought with them the idea of serving hot dogs enhanced with a chili-style sauce. The clever advertising ploy attracted customers who wanted to try the New York–style sandwich. By the early 1930s, Providence boasted a thriving New York System wiener business; Barry Popik confirmed the term was commonly used by eateries in the 1931 *Providence City Directory* while a few other restaurants used the term *Coney Island.*

North Country "Michigan Dogs"

The North Country of New York is the northeastern-most area of the state that includes the Lake Champlain–Adirondack Mountain region and the small city of Plattsburgh. This is the home of the "Michigan," a hot dog served with a sauce that's definitely related to the Greek-sauced Coney Island genre. Folks in those parts debated the origin of Michigans for years, but it wasn't until Gordie Little, radio personality and contributor to Plattsburgh's *Press-Republican,* and Plattsburgh City Clerk Keith Herkalo put their noses to the scent that the story was pieced together.

Herkalo and Little confirmed that Mrs. Eula Otis introduced the Michigan to folks in the North Country. She first served them at her stand on Route 9 South in Plattsburgh in 1925. By 1927, the Otis' "Michigan Hot Dog and Sandwich Shoppe" was open for business in the Plattsburgh Theater Building, and a later announcement heralded the "Opening of the Michigan Hot-Dog Stand Tuesday, May 24, located between the two dance halls, Lake Shore Road, Management of Otis and Quigley, Same Management as 1925."

No one knows where Mrs. Otis got the idea for her special hot dog sauce nor exactly why she called her variation of a frank served with sauce a "Michigan." Many theories have been proposed, but not one has been confirmed. Certainly, Michigan's Coney Island hot dog businesses, such as American Coney Island, founded in 1917, and Todoroff's Original Coney Island, founded in 1914, were well established prior to the time that Mrs. Otis opened her first stand in 1925. Perhaps Mrs. Otis hailed from Michigan or visited the state at some point, or maybe she heard about the Coney Island sauce so popular on hot dogs in Michigan from friends, relatives, or traveling salesmen. While the mystery may never be solved, Mrs. Otis's legacy to North Country cuisine lives on.

Chicago-style Hot Dogs

The Chicago-style hot dog represents a major departure from the typical franks that emerged as a result of immigrants passing through New York. Hot dog researcher Bruce Kraig says the Chicago-style hot dog is based on Hungarian-style sausage, introduced there in the 1920s. According to Kraig, the distinctive Chicago dog was developed as a result of competition around 1920 when Greek and Italian vendors would load up their hot dogs with more and more condiments in order to differentiate themselves from one another. Fluky's, established in 1929 by greengrocer Abe Drexler, claims to be the home of the original Chicago-style hot dog. Drexler converted his vegetable cart into a mobile hot dog stand and sold his vegetable-laden dogs during the 1930s. He also sold a side of french fries for a nickel each. The Fluky's hot dog was called a "depression sandwich."

Many of the clever ways in which hot dogs are now served throughout America are provided in the following chapters. It's likely they will become part of our ever-increasing repertoire of hot dog cuisine and legend.

CHAPTER 2

Hot Dogs of the Northeast: Pushcarts Roll and Mustard Rules

Jayne Mansfield celebrating her reign as Miss National Hot Dog Convention.

The Northeastern region of the United States is pure heaven for hot dog fans. Connecticut, New Jersey, and New York are considered the "Holy Trinity of Tube Steaks," although anyone from Chicago would hotly debate this claim. Pushcarts selling hot dogs abound, especially in major cities like New York. The hands-down favorite condiment is mustard. The sheer variety of hot dogs is mind-boggling, ranging from New York's "Michigans" to Coneys; boiled to deep-fried; and everything in between.

Connecticut

Blackie's Hot Dog Stand

2200 Waterbury Road, Cheshire, CT 06410

(203) 699-1819

Blackie's has been around since 1928. It started out as a gas station but the owners soon discovered that their hot dogs were the big attraction. The gas pumps were removed, and Blackie's has been famous as a top hot dog spot ever since. Hummel Brothers in New Haven, Connecticut, manufactures the all-beef, kosher-style dogs used at Blackie's, which are deep-fried in oil until their sides split open, exposing the juicy interior. Blackie's makes their own mustard, which is mighty good, but their spicy hot relish is absolutely outstanding. A closely guarded secret, fans are left speculating as to the formula for what appears to be a mixture of chopped green peppers, vinegar, and spices—including, perhaps, a bit of cinnamon. There's no sauerkraut, no chili, and no fries—simply because they aren't deemed necessary. Blackie's is closed on Fridays, a tradition said to have originated back in the days when Catholics weren't permitted to eat meat on Fridays.

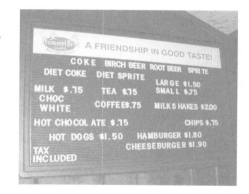

Deep-fried Dogs with Mustard and Pear-Pepper Relish

This mild, delicious relish is a cousin to that served at Blackie's; if more heat is desired, increase the amount of jalapeño peppers. The recipe is adapted from a formula for pear relish shared by the late Chet Beckwith of Baton Rouge, Louisiana, and as Chet would say, "It will set your toes to tapping."

Pear-Pepper Relish

4 firm Bartlett pears, peeled, cored, and coarsely
    ground in a food processor
2 large onions, chopped
2 medium green bell peppers, cored, seeded, and diced
1 medium red bell pepper, cored, seeded, and diced
1 jalapeño pepper (or more, to taste), seeded, deveined,
    and diced
Boiling water
1 1/2 cups sugar
2 1/4 teaspoons mustard seed
3/4 teaspoon ground allspice
1/4 teaspoon ground cinnamon
3/4 teaspoon turmeric
1 tablespoon salt
1 1/2 cups white vinegar

Prepare and place, in three separate bowls, the pears, onions, and all the peppers. Place pears in a colander and pour boiling water over them; drain well and place in a heavy medium pot. Repeat with the onions and then the peppers, adding both to the pot with the pears. Mix the pears and vegetables together. In a medium bowl, combine the sugar, spices, and salt, and add to the pear mixture. Add the vinegar and mix well. Over medium-high heat, bring the mixture to a boil. Reduce the heat to low and simmer, uncovered and stirring occasionally, for 30 minutes. Pour the hot relish into hot, sterilized jars and cover, following the manufacturer's directions for preparation and safety. Process the jars of relish in a boiling hot water bath for 20 minutes. Remove from water and set the jars on kitchen towels to seal; this will be indicated by a popping noise. Yield: about 4 (12-ounce) jars.

Assembly

Canola oil for deep-frying
Hot dogs, all-beef or a pork-and-beef mixture
Hot dog buns, toasted
Spicy brown mustard
Pear-Pepper Relish

In a heavy, deep pot, heat the canola oil over high heat to 350 degrees. Deep-fry the hot dogs, a few at a time, to the desired degree of doneness. Place hot dogs on buns and top with mustard and Pear-Pepper Relish. Serve immediately.

Source:
Hummel Brothers will ship orders for their hot dogs via FedEx.

Hummel Brothers, Inc.
180 Sargent Drive
New Haven, CT 06511
(203) 787-4113

Rawley's Drive-In

1886 Post Road, Fairfield, CT 06824

(203) 259-9023

Rawley's is a busy place, often frequented by famous people like Meg Ryan or David Letterman who have to wait in line like everyone else, and they know it's well worth the wait. Roessler's beef-and-pork franks are first deep-fried in hot oil, then they're slapped onto a hot griddle where any excess oil drains off. With this method, they become delightfully crispy and blistered. The rolls are buttered and toasted on the griddle, and the dogs are served with a choice of toppings. Many fans favor one with "The Works": mustard, sauerkraut, chopped raw onion, and crumbled bacon. The bacon topping is so popular that Rawley's fries up twenty pounds of it every day, and some folks order "heavy bacon," or double the amount.

Bacon-Kraut Dogs

Canola oil for deep-frying
Beef-and-pork franks
Hot dog buns
Butter
Mustard
Sauerkraut, plain or heated (see page 38)
Chopped onion
1 slice bacon per hot dog (or more, to taste),
　　cooked crisp, drained, and crumbled

In a heavy, deep pot, heat the canola oil to 350 degrees. Deep-fry the hot dogs, a few at a time, until they are just beginning to blister. Meanwhile, heat a griddle. As the hot dogs are removed from the oil, transfer them to the griddle and cook until crispy and blistered. Open hot dog buns and lightly butter the inside; place on griddle to toast. Place hot dogs in buns and top with mustard, sauerkraut, onion, and bacon. Serve immediately.

Doogie's

2525 Berlin Turnpike, Newinton, CT 06111

(860) 666-1944

doogieshotdogs.com

Super Duper Weenie

306 Black Rock Turnpike, Fairfield, CT 06430

(203) 334-DOGS

www.superduperweenie.com

Maine

Flo's Famous Steamed Hot Dogs

Route 1, Cape Neddick, ME 03802

www.floshotdogs.com

Don't blink or you'll miss it. Flo's is a tiny, low-ceiling red shack with a tarpaper roof on Route 1 between York and Ogunquit, Maine. Florence Stacey, known for her wit and sass, opened the stand back in 1959. Flo reigned over the business until her death in 2000, at the age of 92, even though she sold it to her son John and his wife, Gail, in 1973. Even the signage at Flo's reflects her direct, no nonsense, downeast attitude: "Prices subject to change according to customer's attitude." Customers tend to mind their manners at Flo's or bear a lashing from Gail's equally sharp tongue. Proper conduct includes ordering only dogs—there's nothing else and no need to ask, either. Customers in queue state the number of dogs they want (most order two or three since they average about three bites each), then, when prompted, they must quickly state desired condiments; no changes are allowed. The special, dubbed a "Flo dog" by devotees, is a steamed dog in a steamed New England–style top-loading bun covered with a narrow ribbon of mayonnaise, Flo's legendary secret hot sauce, and a quick sprinkling of celery salt. Jane and Michael Stern describe the sauce as "a devilishly dark sweet/hot relish of stewed onions, glistening with spice." It's said that the sauce includes molasses. Those who want a bit more bite to their dog request mustard rather than mayo.

Maine Hot Dogs

Although Flo's onion sauce can't be duplicated, this combination of toppings delivers a really tasty weenie. Don't leave out the mayonnaise as it's a favorite topping in Maine for a good reason.

Onion Sauce

1 1/2 tablespoons butter
1 medium onion, chopped
1/3 cup K.C. Original Barbecue Sauce
1/8 teaspoon crushed red pepper flakes
1 tablespoon water

In a small saucepan, melt butter over medium heat and add onion. Lower heat and sauté, stirring occasionally, about 20 to 25 minutes, or until onion is soft and translucent. Stir in barbecue sauce, red pepper flakes, and water. Cook over low heat for 5 minutes. Serve warm. Yield: 1/2 cup.

Assembly

Beef-and-pork hot dogs, steamed or grilled
Hot dog buns, steamed or toasted
Onion Sauce
Mayonnaise
Mustard
Chopped onion
Celery salt

Place hot dogs in warm buns and add Onion Sauce, mayonnaise, mustard, chopped onion, and a sprinkling of celery salt. Serve immediately.

Source: To order Flo's Original Sauce, go to www.floshotdogs.com.

Wasses Hot Dogs

2 N. Main Street, Rockland, ME 04841

(207) 594-7472

www.midcoastmaine.net/wasses

Folks in Maine's Midcoast region rave about Wasses Hot Dogs, and visitors who stop by one of Wasses' locations leave with fond memories of their tasty dogs. Keith Wass established the business in 1972 when he was a college student looking for a summer job. He spotted a hot dog stand for sale and bought it, then set out to differentiate his hot dogs and came up with a formula for cooking them in peanut oil on a griddle, along with onions, that renders a fragrant and delicious crunchy-skinned dog. The Wasses special is served with fried onions, mustard, and relish.

Bacon Cheese Dogs with Fried Onions

Peanut oil
Pork-and-beef hot dogs
Chopped onions
Hot dog buns, steamed
Cheddar cheese, grated and melted in the microwave
1 slice bacon per hot dog, fried crisp and drained

Heat a griddle and add a light coating of peanut oil. Grill the dogs on one side of the griddle while frying the onions on the other side. As the grilling progresses, add more oil if required. When cooked to the desired degree, place the hot dogs in the buns, top with the fried onions, melted cheddar cheese, and bacon. Serve immediately.

Poutine

French fries served with gravy, chili, cheese, and other toppings are a popular side for hot dogs in the Northeast, but in the New England states folks are partial to a French Canadian specialty called *poutine.* It's said that the word derives from the English word *pudding,* but today it's used more as a slang term meaning "mess." Hot crispy french fries are mixed with fresh cheddar cheese curds and topped with piping hot gravy, delivering a delicious dish that is guaranteed to clog the arteries. An Italian-style version of poutine calls for fries topped with cheese curds and meaty spaghetti sauce. Although poutine isn't typically found at hot dog stands (yet), anyone who loves fries will surely want to give it a try.

Massachusetts

Blue Light Kitchens

225 Commerce Street, Provincetown, MA 02657

(508) 487-3466

Blue Light Kitchens hasn't been the recipient of much hoopla among fervent frank fanatics even though it has a terrific roster of hot dogs on its menu. Thankfully, the intrepid Holly Moore ferreted out the place and put it on his website www.hollyeats.com. Blue Light Kitchens serves all-beef Boar's Head hot dogs in freshly baked focaccia that's sliced to resemble the typical New England–style top-loading bun. The dogs are served with an interesting and tasty array of toppings such as the "Hottie" (chili, pepper jack cheese, and sour cream), the Nor'Easter (maple baked beans and bacon), and the yummy "Yodeler." New England regional side dishes include homey macaroni and cheese or baked beans in addition to griddle fries, potato salad, and coleslaw.

Yodeler-Style Hot Dogs

2 all-beef hot dogs, steamed or grilled

2 pieces freshly baked focaccia, sliced or 2 hot dog buns, heated in the oven

1/4 to 1/2 cup grated Swiss cheese

4 ounces fresh mushrooms, sliced and sautéed in 1 1/2 tablespoons butter

Place hot dogs in focaccia or hot dog buns and divide the Swiss cheese and sautéed mushrooms between the two. Serve immediately. Serves 2.

Hot Dog Annie's

244 Paxton Street, Leicester, MA 01524

(508) 892-9059

Hot Dog Annie's is known as "the legend of Leicester." It was established in 1949, and loyal patrons from near and far head out on Route 56, converging on the old-fashioned, tiny, cramped hot dog stand in search of the justifiably famous barbecue hot dogs. The small dogs are grilled and served with a secret, sweet (no-meat) onion barbecue sauce. While some like their dogs with onion, mustard, and relish, others go for "The Ultimate," topped with barbecue sauce, cheese, and onions.

Barbecue Meat Sauced Hot Dogs

Hot Dog Annie's secret barbecue sauce doesn't contain any meat, but this sauce is a great topping for your favorite frank.

Barbecue Meat Sauce

1 tablespoon olive oil

1 large onion, chopped

2 pounds (80 percent lean) ground beef

4 cloves garlic, chopped

1/2 cup ketchup

1 cup smoky, tomato-based barbecue sauce, such as Dinosaur Bar-B-Que Sauce

1 tablespoon hot red pepper sauce, such as Frank's Red Hot Sauce

2 tablespoons plain yellow mustard

In a deep, 10-inch frying pan, heat the olive oil and sauté the onion over medium heat just until it starts to soften. Crumble the beef into the pan and stir with a slotted spoon to break it up as much as possible. Cook beef and onions over low heat, continuing to stir with the slotted spoon, just until beef is lightly browned.

Add the garlic and cook for 1 minute longer. Add remaining ingredients and mix well. Cook, uncovered, over low heat for 25 to 30 minutes, stirring occasionally, until sauce is thick. This sauce freezes well for one month. Yield: 5 cups.

Assembly

Hot dogs, grilled

Hot dog buns, toasted

Barbecue Meat Sauce

Grated cheddar cheese

Chopped onion

Place grilled hot dogs on the toasted buns. Top with Barbecue Meat Sauce, cheese, and onion. Serve immediately.

Source: If Dinosaur Bar-B-Que Sauce isn't available at your local market, it can be ordered at www.dinosaurbarbque.com.

Moogy's Breakfast & Sandwich Shop

154 Chestnut Hill Avenue, Brighton, MA 02155

(617) 254-8114

www.moogys.com

Fries served with gravy are often called "wet fries" in Massachusetts. At Moogy's in Brighton, Massachusetts, owners Philip and Scott Shaffer serve up several varieties of french fries ranging from Crab Fries with Old Bay seasoning to Pizza Fries to Chive Fries with a side of ranch dressing for dipping.

Pizza Fries

1 pound french fries, cooked crispy
2 cups grated mozzarella cheese
Freshly grated Parmesan cheese, to taste
Crushed red pepper, to taste (optional)
1/2 to 1 cup warm pizza sauce

Preheat broiler. Place hot, cooked fries on a baking sheet and top with mozzarella cheese. Place under broiler until cheese melts. Remove fries from broiler and place on a platter. Sprinkle with Parmesan cheese and crushed red pepper, if desired. Serve with warm pizza sauce drizzled over the top or on the side for dipping. Serves 4.

More cool dogs in Massachusetts

George's Coney Island

158 Southbridge Street, Worcester, MA 01608

(508) 753-4362

www.coneyislandlunch.com

Nick's Nest

1597 Northampton Street, Holyoke, MA 01040

(413) 532-5229

New Hampshire

Gilley's PM Lunch

175 Fleet Street, Portsmouth, NH 03801

(603) 431-6343

www.gilleyspmlunch.com

Like many of America's famous hot dog stands, Gilley's
PM Lunch has a lot of history behind it. Gilley's started
out as a horse-drawn lunch cart in 1912. In later years, a diner with a curved wooden roof, manufactured in
1940 by the Worcester Diner Company of Massachusetts, replaced the old cart. It was pulled first by tractor
and later by truck into Portsmouth's Market Square every evening. Gilley's claims to have made the *Guinness
Book of World Records* for the most parking tickets; each evening, the owner would be ticketed for parking in the
square, but because the little diner was so popular, he simply considered the tickets as a cost of doing business.
The diner is named for an employee, Ralph "Gilley" Gilbert, who served hot dogs and hamburgers to patrons
for more than fifty years. It was moved to its present location in 1974. The menu is simplistic, consisting of hot
dogs, burgers, fried egg sandwiches, chili, beans, and french fries. Current owners Steve and Gina Kennedy say
most folks opt for their dogs with "The Works"—which includes mustard, relish, and onion, but ketchup can
be added by ordering the dog "Loaded"—and it also comes "Loaded with Pickles and Mayo."

Loaded with Pickles and Mayo

Pork-and-beef hot dogs, grilled
Hot dog buns, toasted
Mustard
Mayonnaise
Ketchup
Relish

Chopped onion
Pickles

Place hot dogs in toasted buns. Top with mustard,
mayonnaise, ketchup, relish, onion, and pickles. Serve
immediately.

New Jersey

Although Coney Island in Brooklyn, New York, may be credited as the cradle of the American hot dog, and New Yorkers have certainly embraced the tube steak in myriad forms, New Jersey takes a backseat to no one when it comes to wonderful weenies. Frankly speaking, the longtime rivalry between New York and New Jersey can get red hot when it comes to the subject of tube steaks. Folks in the Garden State take their hot dogs very seriously, and they endlessly debate the best kind of hot dog and where to get it. New Jersey aficionado and hot dog expert John Fox flatly states that Jersey is the "hot dog capital of the world . . . serving a wide diversity of hot dogs ranging from Texas weiners, Italian hot dogs, Kosher-style all-beef, New Jersey deep-fried . . . and quality beef pork griddle franks." Philadelphian Holly Moore, whose hot dog website serves as a definitive guide to great dogs, pretty much agrees when he states, "North Jersey, and not Chicago, might well be the hot dog capital of the world." New Jersey is indeed hot dog heaven, and it was a difficult task to narrow down all the available choices to the New Jersey eateries featured here.

Jersey's Italian Hot Dogs and Texas Weiners

John Fox states that New Jersey enjoys two very distinct styles of dogs, and both originated in the state in the 1920s. An Italian hot dog is a deep-fried, all-beef, skinless frank (usually Best brand) that's served on a half of a circular pizza bread, similar to a pita; a double Italian includes two hot dogs.

The New Jersey Texas Weiner is a bit more complicated because there are two variations. The "Hot Texas Weiner" of Paterson, New Jersey, is a deep-fried pork-and-beef dog, usually made by Thumann's, topped, in strict order, by spicy, ballpark-style mustard, chopped onions, and a beanless chili sauce. The "Texas Weiner" from the area around Plainfield, New Jersey, is based on a Grote & Weigle pork-and-beef frank cooked on a griddle and served with a thicker chili sauce. The spelling of "weiner" is also pretty much limited to the New Jersey area.

Charlie's Famous Italian Hot Dogs

18 South Michigan Avenue, Kenilworth, NJ 07033

(908) 241-2627

Charlie's comes highly recommended by nearly every Italian hot dog guru in New Jersey. Charlie Fiorenza established this landmark neighborhood spot back in the early 1960s. Charlie's concentrates on producing top-notch deep-fried Italian dogs topped with quality fresh ingredients, and everything is cooked to order. The single Italian dogs are served on quarter wedges of hearth-baked "pizza bread" while the double Italian dogs are served on a half wedge of bread; they're garnished with onions, red and green peppers, and thin, crispy potatoes that are also deep-fried.

New Jersey Italian Hot Dogs (aka "Newark Hot Dog")

The "pizza bread" used for the Italian hot dog is typically made from left-over pizza dough.

Pizza Bread

Olive oil (not extra virgin)
1 pound prepared, refrigerated pizza dough

Lightly oil a large mixing bowl. Place dough in the bowl and turn to lightly coat. Cover with a towel and set in a warm place for 1 hour. Preheat oven to 350 degrees. On a lightly floured board, punch dough down, shape into a circle about 1 inch in thickness, and let it rest for 15 minutes. Place the round on a baking sheet lightly brushed with olive oil. Lightly brush the dough with olive oil and bake for about 30 minutes, or until the crust is golden brown and the bread sounds hollow when tapped with the fingers. Remove from oven and let cool for at least 15 minutes. Vertically cut bread in half and remove some of the interior bread in each half, forming a pita-like shell. Serves 2.

Assembly

Canola oil for deep-frying
1 large onion, cut in half, then in eighths and separated
1 red bell pepper, seeded and cut in 1-inch pieces
1 green bell pepper, seeded and cut in 1-inch pieces
1 unpeeled medium russet potato, cut in very thin slices
2 all-beef hot dogs
2 Pizza Bread halves
Marinara sauce, heated (optional)

In a deep pot, heat the oil to 350 degrees. Place vegetables in a wire basket and carefully lower into the hot oil. Fry until tender and crispy. Remove from oil and keep warm on a tray lined with paper towels. Reheat the canola oil to 350 degrees. Carefully place the hot dogs in the oil and deep-fry until they are well browned. Remove from oil, place each in Pizza Bread half, and garnish with the vegetables. Top with marinara sauce if desired and serve immediately. Serves 2.

Hot Grill

699 Lexington Avenue, Clifton, NJ 07011

(973) 772-6000

www.thehotgrill.com

The sign outside the Hot Grill advertises the "World's Tastiest Texas Weiners" and indeed, many folks agree that this restaurant is one of the finest places to enjoy a truly traditional Paterson, New Jersey–style Hot Texas Weiner. Greek and Italian immigrants founded the business in 1961, and over the years, celebrities and regular folks have found their way through the doors of this establishment, which has continued to modernize and grow to accommodate the crowds. The deep-fried Sabrett beef-and-pork

dogs are typically ordered "All the Way" and they arrive topped with the Hot Grill's excellent chili sauce, mustard, and finely chopped fresh onion. The homemade chili sauce is sold "to go" by the pint and quart. Although hot dogs are the big seller, the roast beef with gravy platter is nothing to be sneezed at, and it most likely accounts for the fact that the Hot Grill serves some of the best french fries topped with gravy (and/or chili and cheese) to be had anywhere. The Hot Grill's gravy is a bit different, resembling brown gravy with a few ladles of tomato sauce added, a perfect side for a great hot dog.

Fries with Cheese and Tomato-Laced Gravy

1 jar (12 ounces) beef gravy
2 tablespoons plain spaghetti sauce, such as Ragu
1/8 teaspoon garlic powder
1/3 teaspoon ground black pepper
Pinch of dried basil
Pinch of dried oregano
1 1/2 pounds french fries, cooked crispy
1 1/2 cups grated cheddar cheese or cheese of choice

In a small saucepan, combine gravy, spaghetti sauce, garlic powder, black pepper, basil, and oregano, and simmer over low heat for 5 minutes. Preheat broiler. Place fries on a baking sheet and sprinkle with the cheese. Broil until cheese is melted and hot. Remove from broiler, place on a serving platter, and top with the gravy to taste. Serve immediately. Serves 6.

Maui's Dog House

806 New Jersey Avenue, North Wildwood, NJ 08260

(609) 846-0444

www.mauisdoghouse.com

Mike D'Antuono's gourmet hounds have definitely fetched a winning spot in the state's hot dog hall of fame. The franks are made from a secret recipe that Mike inherited from his grandfather; one is a spicy, smoky veal-and-pork mixture that looks like bockwurst, and the other is a milder German frank made from beef and pork. Among the many breeds of dogs offered, the "Drunk" is topped with sauerkraut cooked in micro-brewed beer and spicy German mustard; the "Irish" sports freshly cooked potatoes and a killer blended mayo; and the "Beachcomber" features a mixture of coleslaw, mustard, and pickles. One of the most enticing dogs is the "Soprano," which delivers a creative mixture that packs a walloping good taste; at one time, it was topped with broccoli rabe, but spinach is now used. First timers always get a kick out of the fact that Maui's weenies are served in dog bowls.

Soprano Dogs Like Maui's

High-quality, spicy hot dogs or Italian sausages are excellent served in this manner.

Sautéed Spinach

1 pound spinach, stemmed and washed
1 tablespoon extra virgin olive oil
2 cloves garlic, finely chopped
1 tablespoon dry white wine, such as Chablis (optional)

Place the drained but still wet spinach in a large pot and cook, covered, over low heat just until wilted. Drain the spinach well in a colander, then squeeze out remaining liquid using paper towels. Heat the olive oil over medium heat in a medium frying pan, add garlic, and cook for 30 seconds. Add the spinach and toss it gently with the olive oil and garlic. Add the wine (if using), heat for 1 minute, and serve hot. Yield: about 1 cup.

Assembly

Hot dogs or sausages, grilled
Hot dog buns, toasted
Sautéed Spinach
1 to 2 tablespoons grated provolone cheese per dog

Preheat broiler. Place hot dogs or sausages in buns, and top with Sautéed Spinach and cheese. Place the hot dogs under the broiler just until cheese is melted and serve immediately.

Rutt's Hut

417 River Road, Clifton, NJ 07014

(973) 779-8615

Rutt's Hut may well be the most famous hot dog eatery in New Jersey, and it's certainly the quintessential New Jersey dog experience. Rutt's is a Jersey culinary landmark, established in the early 1940s by Royal (Roy) Rutt. Of course, Rutt's uses the Thumann's beef-and-pork franks that are specially formulated for deep-frying, but this place takes the cooking method to new heights. Rutt's offers four types of dogs that vary in degree of doneness: the "in-and-outer," which is briefly cooked and retains its pink plumpness; the popular "ripper," which is deep-fried until the skin rips open up the side; the "weller," which is well done; and the "cremator," which is deep-fried until black and crispy. The founder's wife developed Rutt's signature condiment, a bright yellow sweet-hot relish, still made from a top-secret recipe.

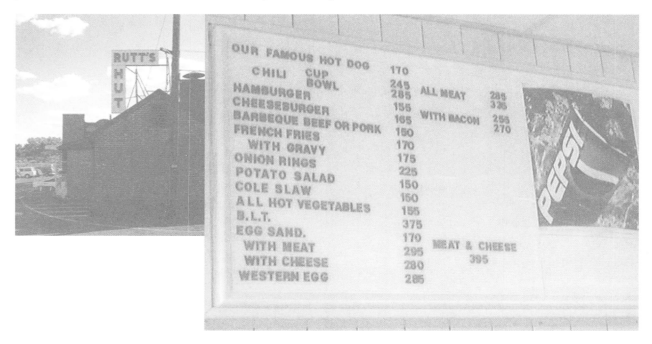

Rippers with Cabbage and Carrot Mustard Slaw

This is not Rutt's secret relish recipe, but it's a very tasty topping for hot dogs. It's adapted from a recipe for mustard slaw in *The Rosengarten Report* by David Rosengarten.

Cabbage and Carrot Mustard Slaw

1 pound cabbage, finely grated

1/3 cup minced green bell pepper

1/2 cup finely grated onion

1/4 cup finely grated carrot

1 teaspoon celery seed

1/2 teaspoon salt

1/2 teaspoon ground black pepper

2 tablespoons freshly squeezed lemon juice

1/2 cup plain yellow mustard, such as French's

1/3 cup sugar

1 tablespoon cider vinegar

1 tablespoon Frank's Red Hot Sauce

In a medium mixing bowl, combine all ingredients and mix well. Cover and refrigerate at least 1 hour before serving. Yield: about 3 cups.

Assembly

Canola oil for deep-frying

Thumann's deep-fry beef-and-pork franks or another brand of beef-and-pork hot dog

Hot dog buns, steamed or toasted

Cabbage and Carrot Mustard Slaw

In a heavy, deep pot, heat the canola oil to 350 degrees. Cook the hot dogs, a few at a time, until the skin rips open up the side. Place hot dogs in the buns, top with Cabbage and Carrot Mustard Slaw, and serve immediately.

More Cool Dogs in New Jersey

Charlie's Pool Room
1122 East Boulevard, Alpha, NJ 08865
(908) 454-1364

Dickie Dee's Pizza
380 Bloomfield Avenue, Newark, NJ 07107
(973) 483-9396

Father & Son Luncheonette
10 E. Blancke Street, Linden, NJ 07036
(908) 486-9596

Hiram's Roadstand
1345 Palisades Avenue, Fort Lee, NJ 07024
(201) 592-9602

Johnny & Hanges
23-20 Maple Avenue, Fair Lawn, NJ 07410
(201) 791-9060

Libby's Lunch
98 McBride Avenue, Paterson, NJ 07501
(973) 278-8718

New York

Coney Island is where America's hot dog tradition really took off. New York has spawned a huge number of fabulous hot dog eateries offering a mind-boggling variety of franks that range from the "dirty water dogs" of street cart vendors to the new emporiums of "haute dogs" that have sprung up throughout the area. Meanwhile, New York boasts hundreds of hot dog establishments, many of which have a rich history dating back many years.

Manhattan and Brooklyn Eateries

Crif Dogs

113 St. Marks Place, New York, NY 10009

(212) 614-2728

Crif Dogs in New York City's East Village falls into the pedigreed category of late-night doghouses, and it features some truly stylish new versions of the hot dog. The slightly risqué sign featuring a naked wiener and the words "Eat Me" easily identifies Crif's. Founders Kerry Kramer and Brian Shebairo base many of their offerings on the same special Thumann's dog, made for deep-frying, that has been used at Rutt's Hut in New Jersey for years, but wrapping each hot dog in bacon before immersion in the deep fryer adds a new dimension. For those who seek glamour in hot dogs, the menu offers exciting bacon-wrapped choices like the Chihuahua dog topped with avocado, sour cream, and salsa; the Tsunami topped with teriyaki, pineapple, and green onions; and the BLT.

Crif-style BLT Dogs

Canola oil for deep-frying

Thumann's hot dogs for deep-frying or substitute
    another brand of pork-and-beef frank

1 slice bacon per hot dog

Hot dog buns, heated

Mayonnaise

Lettuce

Fresh chopped tomato

In a heavy, deep pot, heat canola oil to 350 degrees. Wrap each dog in bacon. Deep-fry the hot dogs, two or three at a time, until dogs and bacon are browned and sizzling. Place hot dogs in heated buns and garnish with mayonnaise, lettuce, and tomato. Serve immediately.

Nathan's Famous

1310 Surf Avenue, Coney Island, Brooklyn, NY 11224

(718) 946-2202

www.nathansfamous.com

Ultimately, all true hot dog lovers make the pilgrimage to historic Nathan's Famous, located on Coney Island's boardwalk since 1916. Patrons whose appetites are fueled by saltwater breezes are lured to the sprawling Nathan's by the pervasive aromas of hot dogs and fries, and hardly anyone is ever disappointed. Nathan's is an American institution, and its all-beef dog is an American icon. The grilled hot dogs are served in soft, steamed buns, and those in the know generally order them New York–style, topped with mustard and sauerkraut.

In an era when chicken was an expensive luxury, Nathan's Famous sold hot dogs in the early twentieth century for a nickel each, thus coining the term "Coney Island Chicken."

The Original Nathan's Famous Hot Dog

Nathan's hot dogs are topped with plain, raw sauerkraut, but if preferred, you can always serve your dogs with the heated version featured on the next page.

Nathan's Famous all-beef hot dogs, grilled
Hot dog buns, steamed
Nathan's Original Coney Island Deli Style Mustard
Sauerkraut, plain or heated (see page 38)

Place the grilled hot dogs in steamed buns and top with mustard and sauerkraut. Serve immediately.

Source: Nathan's Beef Franks are now available in supermarkets throughout major markets in some 40 states. If the franks are not locally available, they may be ordered from www.hometown-treats.com. Nathan's Original Coney Island Deli Style Mustard can be ordered from www.kitchenetc.com.

Sauerkraut for Hot Dogs

Some folks are partial to plain sauerkraut on their hot dogs, but this version, mild and flavorful, is a truly delicious topping.

1 (2-pound) package refrigerated sauerkraut,
   such as Silver Floss
1/2 cup butter
2 medium onions, chopped
1 (14-ounce) can beef broth
1 cup white wine, such as Chablis, divided

Preheat oven to 350 degrees. In a colander, rinse the sauerkraut under running water and drain well. In a deep, medium frying pan, melt butter over low heat. Add onions and sauté, stirring occasionally, for 20 to 25 minutes or until soft and translucent. Add sauerkraut and mix well. Stir in beef broth and, over medium-high heat, bring just to a boil. Remove from heat and stir in 1/2 cup wine. Pour sauerkraut mixture into a 13 x 9-inch non-reactive baking dish and cover tightly with foil. Bake for 1 hour. Remove sauerkraut from oven, stir in the remaining wine, reseal with foil, and return to the oven for 1 hour longer, or until sauerkraut is golden and most of the liquid has evaporated. Yield: 4 cups.

Hot Dog Eating Contest

The annual Fourth of July International Hot Dog Eating Contest takes place at Nathan's in Coney Island. Although plenty of big, strapping American guys enter the contest, they've been out-dogged by Japanese competitors since 1996. Only Steve Keiner, from New Jersey, managed to capture the much-coveted "Mustard Yellow Belt" in 1999. In 2006, Takeru Kobayashi of Nagano, Japan, devoured 53 and 3/4 hot dogs to snag the title for the sixth straight year—and beat his own world record of 53 1/2 dogs, which he downed in 2004.

Papaya King

179 E. 86th Street, New York, NY 10028

(212) 369-0648

and

121 W. 125th Street, New York, NY 10027

(212) 665-5732

www.papayaking.com

Gus Poulos, a Greek immigrant who arrived in New York City in 1923, founded Papaya King. After vacationing in Florida in the late 1920s, he returned to New York and, in 1932, established a juice store called Hawaiian Tropical Fruits. Hula dancers gyrated on the street outside, enticing passersby to try the exotic beverages. The store, located at 86th Street and Third Avenue, was in a German and Polish neighborhood, and Poulos noted the popularity of sausages among his customers. In 1939, he added frankfurters to his menu, and business boomed. In the 1950s, Gus was affectionately dubbed the "Papaya King," and in the early 1960s, the business name was changed to that moniker. The garlicky beef franks are grilled and served on a toasted bun with a choice of condiments such as sauerkraut or tropical relish, fried onions with or without peppers, fried onions and melted cheese, and cheese and/or chili. Although the combination of garlicky franks and fruit juice may be a bit odd to some folks, New Yorkers are hooked on it, and they smugly point to Papaya King signs advertising the health benefits of the papaya.

Franks with Fried Onions and Melted Cheddar Cheese

1 1/2 tablespoons canola oil
1 large onion, thinly sliced
2 garlicky all-beef frankfurters
Hot dog buns, toasted
1/2 cup grated cheddar cheese, melted

In a medium frying pan, heat the oil over low heat. Add the onion and slowly cook until it's soft and golden brown, about 25 minutes. Meanwhile, slowly grill the hot dogs until cooked through and crispy on the outside. Place the hot dogs in toasted buns, top with the fried onions and melted cheese and serve immediately. Serves 2.

The $19 Kobe Beef Hot Dog

Big spenders in New York encounter an enormous array of the world's finest foods and cuisines, and now those with fat wallets may also enjoy the humble hot dog without embarrassment. The Old Homestead, established in 1868, is a steakhouse located in the heart of the city's Meatpacking District in Chelsea. Home of the $41 Kobe beef hamburger, the Old Homestead also offers a Kobe beef hot dog for a paltry $19. Old Homestead, 56 Ninth Avenue, New York, NY 10011; (212) 807-0707.

New York City Street Carts

Metropolitan New York boasts some 3,000 hot dog vendors. Pushcart vendors range from those offering Sabrett and Hebrew National dogs to the recent upscale carts making a definite impact on New York's hot dog scene. While many of the carts still serve what is affectionately known as "dirty water dogs"—simply because the hot

dogs are boiled in water and sometimes reside in their bath for some time—more and more vendors are selling grilled hot dogs. The carts are located on street corners throughout Manhattan, and long lines of customers formed during the lunch hour often identify the best.

Hebrew National Carts, marked by bright red-and-yellow umbrellas, sell 100 percent pure kosher beef franks. The company was founded in New York's Lower East Side as the Hebrew National Kosher Sausage Factory, Inc. Garlicky Hebrew National franks are sold through retail outlets nationwide, and the corporate website, www.hebrewnational.com, provides a store locator as well as a mail order service for their products.

The Sabrett carts, another New York tradition, sport bright yellow-and-blue umbrellas, and their operators serve up Sabrett's natural casing, all-beef wieners. The boiled dogs are typically topped with mustard, sauerkraut, and/or that famous New York onion sauce.

New York Hot Dog Onion Sauce

The preparation of New York's onion sauce differs from cart to cart, with some versions much thinner than this formula.

1 1/2 teaspoons olive oil
4 large onions, sliced and chopped
1 (11.5-ounce) can V8 Juice
1/2 cup water
1 tablespoon tomato paste
1 1/2 teaspoons sweet Hungarian paprika
1 teaspoon corn syrup
1/2 teaspoon cornstarch
1/4 teaspoon salt
1/2 teaspoon crushed red pepper flakes, or more to taste
3 tablespoons cider vinegar, or more to taste

In a medium pot, heat olive oil over medium heat and add onions. Cook, uncovered, for 10 minutes, stirring frequently. Turn heat to low and sauté onions, stirring frequently, for 30 minutes, or until onions are softened and translucent but not browned. Add remaining ingredients and cook over low heat, uncovered and stirring frequently, for 1 1/2 to 2 hours, or until mixture thickens and onions are very tender. Taste and adjust seasoning, adding more crushed red pepper and vinegar if desired. Yield: about 2 1/2 cups.

Pushcart Pups

All-beef hot dogs, boiled or grilled
Hot dog buns, steamed
Plain yellow mustard
Sauerkraut, plain or heated (see page 38)
New York Hot Dog Onion Sauce

Place hot dogs in buns and top with mustard. Add Sauerkraut and top with New York Hot Dog Onion Sauce. Serve immediately.

Sources: Sabrett hot dogs and condiments, including sauerkraut, relish, spicy brown mustard, and onions in sauce, are available through retail markets or by mail order through the following distributor:

Foods of New York
All County Provisions
66 Peconic Avenue, Medford, NY 11763
(800) HOTDOG-6
www.foodsofnewyork.com

The Tiny Pups of Troy, New York

Famous Lunch

111 Congress Street, Troy, NY 12180

(518) 272-9481

and

Troy Pork Store

158 4th Street, Troy, NY 12180

(518) 272-8291

The city of Troy, New York, was once named Vanderhyden, but in 1789, the name was changed to Troy. Following the Revolutionary War, Americans celebrated their freedom from England and a true sense of democracy as established in Greece centuries earlier. Many towns in New York were named after Greek locations, including Ithaca and Troy. Greek immigrants arrived in New York City at the turn of the twentieth century, and many of them eventually relocated to these cities. Along the way, they became acquainted with hot dogs and the concept of serving them with various meat sauces. Sometimes these hot dogs were called Coney Island hots, some were referred to as Texas hots, and others were given distinctive names by their creators. The chili meat sauces of the Troy area often resemble the distinctive Greek chili sauces served on Coney's in Cincinnati, Ohio.

A case in point is Famous Lunch in Troy, known for its "Zippy-sauced" dogs. Established in 1932 by Greek immigrants, it was first known as the Quick Lunch, specializing in tiny three-and-a-half inch long hot dogs made by the Troy Pork Store, that were served up with a special chili meat sauce, yellow mustard, and chopped onions. In 1954, a young marine pining for a taste of home convinced the United States Embassy in Moscow to procure a shipment of hot dogs from Quick Lunch in celebration of the ambassador's birthday. "Operation Hot Dogs" received national acclaim, and Quick Lunch thereafter became known as Famous Lunch.

Little has changed at this Troy landmark; high wooden booths and paneled walls covered with yellowing photos evoke the nostalgia of yesteryear. Customers typically order at least six, and sometimes a dozen of the spicy little dogs that carry a garlicky punch. They're cooked up on a stainless-steel grill and served on miniature rolls.

Troy Teeny Weenies

Miniature Troy Pork Store hot dogs, grilled
Miniature hot dog buns, or halved standard buns
Chili meat sauce from Famous Lunch or substitute
      Cincinnati Chile (see page 100)
Plain yellow mustard
Chopped onion

Place the grilled hot dogs in buns and top with chili, mustard, and onion. Serve immediately.

Source: Famous Lunch will ship Troy Pork Store hot dogs along with the requisite little buns and its Zippy Hot Dog Sauce in quantities ranging from a pint to a gallon. For information, call (518) 272-9481.

Teeny Weenies and Baby Buns

The Troy Pork Store dates back to 1887 when W. A. Guy opened his meat stall at 158 4th Street. In the early 1930s, local Greek hot dog vendors approached the Troy Pork Store and requested smaller hot dogs because the regular size dogs were too hard for children to eat. That special order resulted in Troy's "teeny weenies." Today, it's owned and operated by Walter Pohlmann, who took over the store in 1964, and he's a veritable treasure trove of history about sausages, hot dogs, and the teeny weenie tradition. The Troy Pork Store sells a full line of delicious sausages, but it's renowned for those diminutive hot dogs, about the same size as brown-and-serve breakfast sausages. Miniature buns are available from Bella-Napoli Italian Bakery (518) 274-8277, or Perrotta's Bakery (518) 283-4711, both in Troy.

Nick Tahou Hots

2260 Lyell Avenue, Rochester, NY 14606

(585) 429-6388

Nick Tahou Hots in Rochester, New York, is a hot dog joint where patrons can enjoy Texas red hots and white pork hots that are split and then fried before they're plopped into buns and served with a variety of condiments, including Nick's spicy chili sauce. But Nick Tahou Hots is also the home of the one and only "Garbage Plate™," an all-encompassing sandwich plate that includes meat and two sides. It's considered de rigueur to head for Nick's after a night on the town—a garbage plate can be a very sobering experience.

Alexander Tahou established Nick's, as it's locally known, in 1918. The original "Garbage Plate" followed shortly thereafter, but at that time, it was called "Hots and Potatoes." In those days, two hot dogs would be accompanied by a choice of either cold baked beans or home fries, a meal that kept many a working man well fed at a reasonable price, especially during the depression.

While the choice of sides was expanded over the years, Nick's continued with the original moniker until the early 1980s when college kids insisted upon ordering "the plate with all that garbage on it." The Tahou's natural resistance to the term *garbage* was finally overcome when they realized its marketability. "Garbage Plate" was trademarked, and word of the unique "sandwich" has spread across the country.

A typical Garbage Plate is usually composed of two red hots or white hots cradled in optional rolls. Diners then have a choice of two sides: home fries, macaroni salad, french fries, or cold or hot baked beans. The plate is then topped off with a few squirts of spicy brown mustard, the Tahous' secret hot chili sauce, and chopped raw onion.

The Dumpster Plate

2 Zweigle's red hots or white hots, grilled (see Source)

2 hot dog buns

Choose 2 of the following sides:

    1/2 cup macaroni salad

    1/2 cup home fries

    1/4 pound french fries

    1/2 cup cold or hot baked beans

Topping

Spicy brown mustard (such as Gulden's)

1 cup chili

Chopped raw onion

Place grilled hot dogs in buns and place on a plate. Add sides of choice. Squirt everything with mustard, top with chili and chopped onion, and serve immediately. Serves 1.

Source: Zweigle's, Inc., has produced Rochester's famous white hots since 1925. Wilhelm Zweigle and his wife, Josephine, established the firm when they opened a small sausage shop in 1880. The white hots are similar to a bratwurst and they're best when slowly grilled. Zweigle's also makes pork-and-beef–filled Texas Brand Red Hots. Both the red and white hots are marketed as "Pop Opens" because during the cooking process, they actually grow to a pudgy size. The company recently introduced Zweigle's Hot Dog Sauce and Zweigle's Honey Brown Mustard, and both are delicious toppings for any frank. If Zweigle products aren't available in your area, Calabresella's in Rochester offers mail order via their website: www.newyorkstyledeli.com.

Disco Fries

In recent years, eateries in the Northeast, including New Jersey, New York, and Connecticut, have listed disco fries on their menus. The trend is heading south to Maryland and Atlanta. But what are they? Disco fries are nothing more than fries with gravy and, usually, cheese. The name puts a new spin on an old favorite, sometimes known by such unglamorous names as dirty fries or wet fries. The gravy can be beef, chicken, or turkey and even the cheese varies from American to cheddar or mozzarella. In some of Northern New Jersey's casual Italian eateries, an order of fries with cheese and gravy will result in fries covered with mozzarella and tomato sauce, known as "red gravy."

Ted's Hot Dogs

2312 Sheridan Drive, Tonawanda, NY 14150

(716) 834-6287

www.tedsonline.com

Western New York is definitely hot dog country, and the preferred method of cooking is charcoal grilled. Years ago, great hots and hot cars could be found at Ted's on Sheridan Drive in Tonawanda, just north of Buffalo. Greek immigrant Theodore Spiro Liaros, who arrived in America in 1913, founded the business. Ted initially operated a horse-drawn hot dog cart in a park adjacent to the construction site of the Peace Bridge designed to span the Niagara River and link Buffalo and Canada. The Sheridan Drive location opened in 1948, followed by other area locations over the years.

Ted's serves charcoal-grilled Sahlen's hot dogs with a choice of toppings, but most folks order them with "The Works," which means mustard, relish, onion, Ted's special hot sauce, and a pickle spear; the condiments are applied by counter employees called "dressers."

Buffalo-style Charcoal-Grilled Hot Dogs

Pork-and-beef hot dogs, grilled
Hot dog buns, toasted on the grill
Red's Hot Dog Sauce (see Sources)
Plain yellow mustard
Sweet pickle relish
Chopped onion
1 dill pickle spear per hot dog

Place hot dogs in buns. Top with hot dog sauce, mustard, relish, onion, and a pickle spear. Serve immediately.

Sources:

Redlinski Meats in Buffalo, New York, sells an excellent hot dog sauce very similar to that served at Ted's. To order Red's Hot Dog Sauce, go to Redlinski's website at www.buffalofoods.com.

Buffalo specialty dogs can be ordered from the following producers:

Sahlen Packing Company, Inc.
318 Howard Street, Buffalo, NY 14206
(716) 852-8677, www.buffalofoods.com

F. Wardynski's & Sons, Inc.
336 Peckham Street
P. O. Box 336, Buffalo, NY 14240
(716) 854-6083, www.wardynski.com

Texas Hot Restaurant

132 N. Main Street, Wellsville, NY 14895

(585) 593-1400

The Texas Hot is probably the most popular eatery in beautiful Allegany County, New York. It's known for terrific "Texas hots," hot dogs served with a delicious ground meat sauce typical of Greek-owned hot dog restaurants and stands. George Raptis and John Rigas established the business in 1921. Still in the original location, third-generation family members Mike Raptis and Chris Rigas now run it. Tobin hot dogs are grilled, tucked into steamed rolls, and topped with the special sauce that has made the Texas Hot Restaurant so famous.

Texas Hot Sauce and Dogs

Many cooks in Allegany County have a copycat recipe for the secret sauce served at the Texas Hot. This is one of the best.

Texas Hot Sauce

1/4 cup butter
1 cup chopped onion
1 pound lean ground beef
1 teaspoon sugar
1 teaspoon ground cloves
1 teaspoon cayenne pepper
1 teaspoon chili powder
1 teaspoon nutmeg
1 teaspoon dry mustard
1 teaspoon paprika
1 teaspoon cinnamon
1 teaspoon Worcestershire sauce
1 teaspoon salt
1 teaspoon ground black pepper

In a medium saucepan, melt butter over medium heat and add onion. Sauté onion until soft but not brown. Add ground beef and spices, and mix well; add enough water to just cover the mixture.

Simmer mixture over low heat, stirring occasionally, until meat is cooked and sauce is thickened, about 30 minutes. Yield: about 3 cups.

Assembly

Hot dogs, grilled
Hot dog buns, steamed
Texas Hot Sauce
Plain yellow mustard
Chopped onion

Place hot dogs in buns and top with Texas Hot Sauce, mustard, and onion. Serve immediately.

Source: Tobin's First Prize hot dogs are available throughout the country. Retail information is available at the following website: www.johnmorrell.com.

North Country "Michigan Dogs"

Michigans are a variation of the Coney Island hot dog, served in the North Country region of New York. They date back to 1925 when the Michigan was first introduced by Mrs. Eula Otis of Plattsburgh. In the mid-1930s, Jack "Nitzi" Rabin (also known as Irving J. Rabinowitz) purchased Mrs. Otis' Little Michigan Hot Dog Stand on Route 9 in Plattsburgh; the transaction included her secret sauce recipe, but the business name was changed to Nitzi's. McSweeney's Red Hots now owns the stand, but the old Nitzi's sign is still there. The following Plattsburgh eateries, among many others, are well known for their Michigans:

McSweeney's Red Hots
4704 State Route 9, Plattsburgh, NY 12901
(518) 561-1133

Clare & Carl's Hot Dog Stand
(a seasonal operation established in 1942)
Route 9 South, Plattsburgh, NY 12901
(518) 561-1163

North Country Michigans

This is an adaptation of a recipe credited to Mrs. Brankman at Clare & Carl's Hot Dog Stand in Plattsburgh, New York.

Michigan Sauce

1 tablespoon vegetable oil
1 medium onion, chopped
2 tablespoons cider vinegar
2 tablespoons light brown sugar
1/4 cup freshly squeezed lemon juice
1 1/2 teaspoons prepared yellow mustard
3 tablespoons Worcestershire sauce
Salt and pepper, to taste
1 cup ketchup
1 pound (80 percent lean) ground beef

In a medium frying pan, heat the oil and sauté the onion over medium heat until it softens. Add all remaining ingredients except the ground beef, stir well, and heat.

Crumble the ground beef into the mixture, stirring well to break up the meat. Simmer over low heat for 30 to 40 minutes, or until mixture thickens. Yield: about 2 cups.

Assembly

Hot dogs, steamed or grilled
Hot dog buns, steamed or toasted
Michigan Sauce
Plain yellow mustard
Chopped onion

Place hot dogs in buns. Top with Michigan Sauce, mustard, and onion. Serve immediately.

More Cool Dogs in New York

F&B Gudt Food

269 W. 23rd Street, New York, NY 10011

(646) 486-4441

www.gudtfood.com

Heid's of Liverpool

305 Oswego Street, Liverpool, NY 13088

(315) 451-0786

www.heidshotdogs.com

Hot Dog Charlie's

626 2nd Avenue, Troy, NY 12182

(518) 235-0488

www.hotdogcharlies.com

Katz's Delicatessen

205 E. Houston Street, New York, NY 10002

(212) 254-2246

Sparky's American Food

135A North 5th Street, Brooklyn, NY 11211

(718) 302-5151

Walter's Hot Dog Stand

937 Palmer Avenue, Mamaroneck, NY 10543

No public phone

www.waltershotdogs.com

Pennsylvania

Pennsylvania is a really great hot dog state. Favorite franks include Coney Island hot dogs served in the Texas wiener manner. In addition to french fries as a great accompaniment, frank fanatics can order a side of pierogies, sometimes described as an Eastern European version of the Italian ravioli.

Original Hot Dog Shop

3901 Forbes Avenue, Pittsburgh, PA 15213

(412) 621-1185

www.originalhotdogshop.com

Sid and Essie Simon opened the Original Hot Dog Shop in Pittsburgh in 1960. The Pittsburgh Pirates were playing at Forbes Field, only a block away, and it didn't take long for the eatery to become a Pittsburgh tradition. Affectionately known as "The O," it's definitely a cool place for great grilled dogs and fries. "O dogs," either beef-and-pork or kosher-style pure beef, are served with a variety of condiments that include cheese, bacon, onion, mustard, relish, pickle, chili, sauerkraut, and mayonnaise. The "hot dog Parmesan" delivers a tasty twist on the traditional dog.

Hot Dog Parmesan

Italian Sauce

1 tablespoon olive oil
1/2 cup chopped green bell pepper
1/2 cup chopped onion
1/2 cup plain spaghetti sauce, such as Ragu Traditional
Pinch of dried oregano
Pinch of dried basil

Heat the oil in a deep frying pan, add bell pepper and onion, and sauté over low heat until softened, about 15 minutes. Stir in spaghetti sauce, oregano, and basil, and simmer over low heat for 15 minutes. Yield: about 1/2 cup.

Assembly

5 hot dogs, grilled
5 hot dog buns, steamed or grilled
Italian Sauce
2 tablespoons grated provolone cheese per dog
Grated Parmesan cheese

Place hot dogs in buns, divide Italian Sauce among them, top with cheeses and serve immediately. Serves 5.

Johnny's Hots

1234 N. Delaware Avenue, Philadelphia, PA 19125

(215) 423-2280

www.johnnyshots.com

Johnny's Hots started out in small, nondescript digs not far from its spiffy new location marked by a sign that denotes his "famous hot sausage." The sausage is great, but so are Johnny's hot dogs. To the delight of Philadelphians, he carries on the tradition of what's locally known as "Philadelphia Surf and Turf" in which a grilled fish cake is split and mashed in with a hot dog and served up on a special bun that resembles an Italian dinner roll.

Philadelphia Surf and Turf

1 hot dog, grilled

1 Italian- or French-style roll, toasted

1 quality frozen fish cake, prepared according to package directions

Plain yellow mustard

Chopped onions

Place the hot dog on the bun. Mash the fish cake a bit and place on top of the hot dog. Serve topped with mustard and onion. Yield: 1 serving.

Note: Non-traditional but very tasty toppings for the Surf and Turf dog include Eastern North Carolina Coleslaw (see page 78) or Tartar Sauce (see below).

Tartar Sauce

Linda Rosser of Bowmansville, New York, has served this tartar sauce for many years. It's definitely addictive.

3/4 cup quality mayonnaise, such as Hellman's

3 tablespoons chopped sweet pickle relish

1 tablespoon dried parsley or 2 tablespoons chopped fresh parsley

2 tablespoons finely chopped onion

2 teaspoons horseradish

In a small bowl, combine all ingredients and mix well. Refrigerate, covered, until ready to serve. Yield: about 1 cup.

Levis Combo

Fourteen-year-old Abe Levis was sent from Lithuania to America to avoid being drafted into the Czar's army for twenty-five years. In 1895, Levis opened a small sandwich shop on Sixth Street in Philadelphia's South Street business district where he sold sandwiches, including hot dogs and fish cakes, ice cream, and Levis Champ Cherry Soda, now owned by Amazing Beverages, Inc. Although Levis Hot Dogs closed in 1992, the "Levis Combo," composed of a hot dog and a mashed fish cake topped with mustard and onions, lives on in the hearts and memories of Philadelphians. For more information, check out this website: www.elliotsamazing.com.

Yocco's Hot Dog King

625 Liberty Street, Allentown, PA 18102

(610) 433-1950

Yocco's Hot Dog King has numerous locations throughout Allentown (including the original on Liberty Street) and the Lehigh Valley region of Pennsylvania. It was founded in 1922 by the Iacocca family, relatives of American industrialist Lee Iacocca who was an Allentown native and son of Italian immigrants. Gary Iacocca, third-generation owner, is now president of Yocco's, known for its hot dogs served with Texas wiener–style sauce. The dogs, previously manufactured by Medford, Inc., and still called a "Medford dog," are now produced by Hatfield Quality Meats, and Yocco's says that it's a specially blended frank developed to optimize the flavor by grilling; it has a distinct spiciness to it. Their secret sauce tops a "Yocco," a well-done Medford dog served in a steamed roll with tangy mustard and chopped onions. They also serve Mrs. T's brand pierogies, which come in those little fast food–style French fry bags—in this case marked "peirogies."

Tastes Like Yocco's Hot Dog with Chili Sauce

This recipe is an adaptation of several recipes found on the Internet that purport to deliver the flavor of Yocco's famous top-secret sauce.

Chili

1 pound (80 percent lean) ground beef
Cold water
1 medium onion, chopped
3 tablespoons chili powder
1 teaspoon salt
3/4 teaspoon dried oregano
3/4 teaspoon ground cumin seed
1/4 teaspoon crushed red pepper flakes
2 cups water

Soak ground beef in cold water for 30 minutes and drain; this ensures that the beef will remain free of lumps and cook up into the proper consistency typical of Coney- and Texas-style sauces. Place drained beef in a medium saucepan, add onion and spices, and mix well. Stir in the 2 cups of water and place over medium heat. Cook the chili, stirring occasionally, for about 1 hour, or until it thickens. The chili may be frozen for up to 3 months. Yield: about 3 1/2 cups.

Assembly

Hot dogs, grilled
Hot dog buns, steamed
Plain yellow mustard
Chili
Chopped onion

Place hot dogs in buns and top with mustard, chili, and onion. Serve immediately.

Source: Hatfield Quality Meats, established in 1895, also produces Phillies Franks and Phillies Beef Franks, the "Official Frank of Citizen's Bank Park," home of the Philadelphia Phillies. The company website provides information on where their products can be purchased.

Hatfield Quality Meats
2700 Funks Road
P.O. Box 902, Hatfield, PA 19440-0902
(800) 523-5291 or (215) 368-2500
www.hatfieldqualitymeats.com

More Cool Dogs in Pennsylvania

Coney Island Lunch
515 Lackawanna Avenue, Scranton, PA 18503
(570) 961-9004
www.texas-wiener.com

Lenny's Hot Dogs
606 West Street Road, Feasterville, PA 19053
(215) 355-7616

Texas Wieners
1426 Snyder Avenue, Philadelphia, PA 19145
(215) 465-8635

Tony Luke's
39 East Oregon Avenue, Philadelphia, PA 19148
(215) 551-5725
www.tonylukes.com

Rhode Island

In Rhode Island, folks typically use the term wiener, not hot dog, and the spelling of wiener varies from one eatery to the next, such as "weiner" or "wiener." The most popular preparation of wieners in Rhode Island includes topping them with sauces similar to the Coney Island fine-grind chili sauces. However, Rhode Island refers to its unique preparation of wieners as the "New York System," indicating that New York was where the sauce originated and that it was subsequently brought to Rhode Island by immigrants opening hot dog eateries.

New York System wieners, also referred to as "hot wieners" or "gaggas" in the local vernacular, are only about four inches in length, and they're cooked slowly on a griddle, then served in equally small steamed buns "All da Way," topped with chopped raw onions, mustard, celery salt, and the distinctive Rhode Island chili-style sauce that writer Paul Lukas, in his *New York Times* article entitled "The Big Flavors of Little Rhode Island," described as "a greasy ground beef sauce that's not quite chili, not quite gravy, distinct unto itself." The grill men used to line as many as a dozen of the tiny wieners up the length of their forearm in order to efficiently apply the toppings, but sanitary codes no longer allow the "up the arm" preparation, and small trays have replaced the old method that provided great entertainment for diners. Of interest is that New York System Hot Wiener Sauce not only includes celery salt but the wieners are finished off with an additional sprinkling of celery salt, the distinctive condiment used in Chicago-style hot dogs.

Original New York System

424 Smith Street, Providence, RI 02908

(401) 331-5349

Gust Pappas founded the Original New York System restaurant in 1927, and it claims to be the first of many such wiener emporiums in Rhode Island. Pappas immigrated to the United States from Greece, and passed through New York City where he first learned about the popularity of hot dogs in America. When Pappas eventually arrived in Providence, he began selling hot dogs from a street cart, and soon after opened his eatery at 424 Smith Street. It was originally named New York System, but after relatives and employees, who apprenticed at Pappas' restaurant, went off and started competing New York System shops, the name was changed to Original New York System. Today, Gust Pappas' grandson Gus runs the business. He points out that the wieners are made from a mixture of pork and veal, accounting for the pale pink color, but adds that the true secret of a New York System wiener is the sauce (and his recipe, of course, is top-secret). Most customers order three or four of the little weenies.

New York System Hot Wiener Sauce

This recipe is adapted from several traditional recipes for Rhode Island's hot wiener sauce. It produces a tasty sauce that gently teases the taste buds. After saucing the hot dogs, be sure to add another sprinkling of celery salt.

1 pound (80 percent lean) ground beef
1 (14-ounce) can beef broth
1/4 cup water
1/2 cup freshly chopped onion
1 1/4 teaspoons paprika
1 1/4 teaspoons ground cumin
1/2 teaspoon salt
1/4 teaspoon celery salt
1/4 teaspoon allspice
1 teaspoon plain yellow mustard
1 tablespoon quality chili powder

In a deep, 10-inch skillet, combine the ground beef with the beef broth and water; stir well with a slotted spoon just until meat breaks up. Add remaining ingredients and bring to a simmer over medium heat, stirring occasionally with a slotted spoon so beef doesn't clump. Simmer, uncovered, for 45 minutes, stirring occasionally, until most of the liquid evaporates but the sauce is still gravy-like. If necessary, lower heat to keep from boiling. Yield: about 3 cups.

Rhode Island Hot Wieners "All da Way"

Pork-and-veal or pork-and-beef wieners
Hot dog buns, steamed
Plain yellow mustard
Chopped onion
New York System Hot Wiener Sauce (see above)
Celery salt

Slowly cook the wieners on a griddle and place them in steamed buns. Top with mustard, onion, and hot wiener sauce, and finish with a dash of celery salt. Serve immediately.

Sources: For grilling, Rhode Islanders favor "Saugies," German-style frank-furters first introduced by Saugy Inc., established in 1869. Saugy takes orders for direct shipment via their website, www.saugy.net, or by phone, (401) 640-1879 or (toll free) 866-GO-SAUGY.

Spike's Junk Yard Dogs

273 Thayer Street, Providence, RI 02906

(401) 454-1459

Rhode Island's signature New York System wieners have traditionally dominated the hot dog market in the state, but not long ago, a new dog showed up in the neighborhood. Created by David Drake and Jordy Writer, Spike's Junk Yard Dogs was founded at the Thayer Street location in Providence, Rhode Island, in 1992, and it's now a rapidly growing regional chain. Spike's claims to serve "the world's best dog, maybe better." The menu features a long list of creative specialties, ranging from "the mutt" (a plain dog) to the Samurai Dog (teriyaki sauce and sautéed onions) and the signature Junk Yard Dog (tomato, pickle, scallions, pepperoncini, and Spike's mustard). Although the Lonely Guy Dog may scare a few patrons off with its topping of Spike's mustard, scallions, chopped onions, and sautéed onions, those who lust after Buffalo chicken wings will undoubtedly opt for the Buffalo Dog. There's even a Dog Gone Veggie Dog comprised of tomato, kraut, onion, salsa, pickle, and pepperoncini. The jumbo all-beef dogs are made in New England, and the rolls are freshly baked in-house throughout the day. The Spike's located at 108 Brighton Avenue in Allston, Massachusetts, really takes its mission to the dogs with its exemplary collection boxes that help support Spike's Emergency Fun. Established to provide medical aid for homeless animals at the Boston SPCA, it's a program that gets four paws up!

Buffalo-style Dog

All-beef hot dogs, grilled
Fresh quality buns, toasted if desired
Original Anchor Bar Buffalo Wing Sauce, to taste
Crumbled blue cheese (about 1 tablespoon per hot dog)
Chopped fresh scallions, including the green
      part, to taste

Place the grilled hot dogs on toasted buns and top with wing sauce, blue cheese, and scallions. Serve immediately.

Source: The Original Anchor Bar Buffalo Wing Sauce, created by Teressa Bellissimo in 1964, can be ordered from the following:

Anchor Bar Restaurant
1047 Main Street
Buffalo, NY 14209
(716) 884-4083
www.buffalowings.com

Vermont

Al's French Frys

1251 Williston Road, South Burlington, VT 05403

(802) 862-9203

www.alsfrenchfrys.com

Al and Genevieve Rusterholz established Al's French Frys in 1947, vending fries from a trailer. Today, Al's is an institution in Burlington, Vermont. The snack bar is known for its burgers and hot dogs as well as its famous fries. Chili dogs, cheese dogs, and corn dogs top the list of favorites. Now about those french fries—between one and two thousand pounds of russet potatoes are cooked up at Al's every day. They're first blanched, then cooked a second time to make them nice and crispy. Some folks like their Al's fries with vinegar or ketchup but the real treat is an order of fries with turkey gravy or cheddar cheese—or both!

Turkey-Cheddar Fries

1/2 pound hot french fries, cooked crispy
Salt and pepper
1 cup grated medium or sharp cheddar cheese
1/2 cup medium-thick hot turkey gravy

Preheat broiler. Spread fries in a single layer on a rimmed baking sheet and add salt and pepper to taste. Sprinkle cheese evenly over fries and place under broiler until cheese melts. Remove from broiler, place on a serving dish, cover with hot gravy and serve immediately. Serves 2 to 3.

Vermont Maple Dogs

This is an adaptation of the Vermont maple hot dog recipe created by the Bennington Potter's Yard, Bennington, Vermont.

1/2 cup real maple syrup (grade B is recommended)
1 teaspoon butter
1 teaspoon soy sauce
6 hot dogs
6 hot dog buns, toasted
Honey mustard
Relish

In a deep, non-stick frying pan, combine syrup, butter, and soy sauce and heat to a simmer. Score hot dogs and add to the simmering sauce, turning them to coat well. Simmer the hot dogs until the sauce is dark and slightly thick and the hot dogs are cooked through, about 10 to 15 minutes. Place hot dogs in toasted buns and serve immediately with honey mustard and relish. Serves 6.

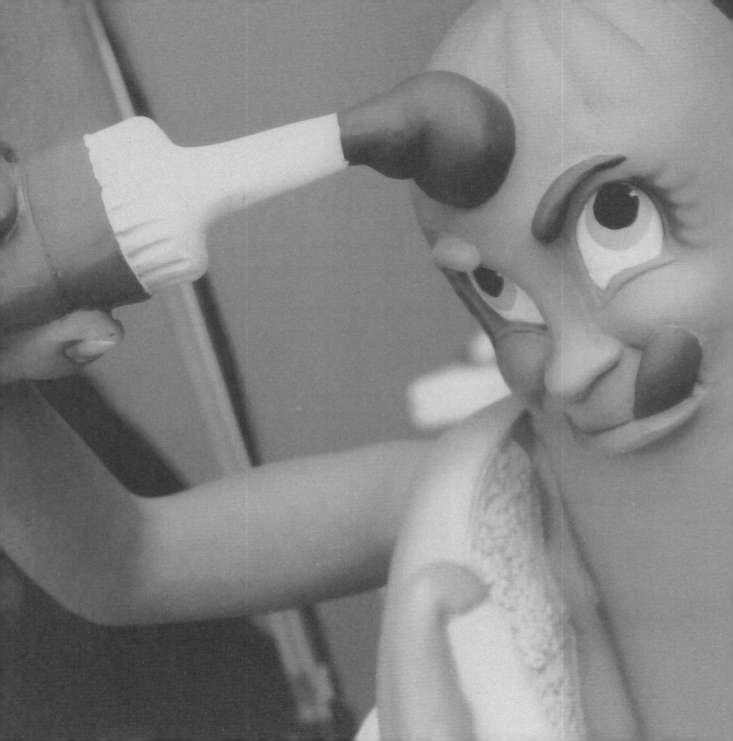

CHAPTER 3

Hot Dogs of the Southeast:
Slaw Dogs and a Slathering of Sauces

Even a trusty trademark savors the regions authentic toppings.

First and foremost, Southerners love their hot dogs topped with coleslaw, which comes in myriad ways: sweet, vinegary, mustard, and barbecue style. Sauces are just as varied, ranging from Coney and chili to the high-falutin' remoulade sauce found on hot dogs in New Orleans. The South features outposts catering to folks pining for a Chicago-style dog or to New Yorkers who need to assuage their hunger for a Nathan's Coney Island frank. True hot dog fans are urged to try the distinct regional specialties such as the Pimiento Cheese Dog, a perennial favorite at The Varsity in Atlanta, or the sometimes daunting Dinglewood-style Scrambled Dog, piled high with chili and loads of condiments.

Alabama

Pete's Famous Hot Dogs

1925 Second Avenue North, Birmingham, AL 35203

(205) 252-2905

Pete's Famous Hot Dogs, established in 1915, is still located in the same tiny shop that measures about 24 feet in length and 8 feet wide. Birmingham recognized the historic eatery in 1998 with a resolution honoring Constantine George "Gus" Koutroulakis who has run the shop since 1948. Crispy grilled hot dogs are served on steamed buns with mustard, onions, coleslaw or sauerkraut, and a secret recipe, meaty chili sauce that manages, in the Birmingham tradition, to be tangy (there's a definite vinegary zing), sweet, and spicy.

Alabama Coney-style Hot Dogs

Alabama Coney Sauce

1 pound (80 percent lean) ground beef

1 medium onion, chopped

2 tablespoons plain yellow mustard

3 tablespoons cider vinegar, or more to taste

1 tablespoon sugar

1/2 cup water

1 1/2 teaspoons Worcestershire sauce

1/4 teaspoon celery seed

1 teaspoon Frank's Red Hot Sauce

1/2 cup tomato sauce

1 cup ketchup

In a medium frying pan over medium-high heat, brown the beef with the onion. As the mixture browns, break up the beef with a fork. Pour off fat and add all remaining ingredients, mixing well.

Simmer over low heat, partially covered and stirring frequently for 1 hour, or until mixture thickens. If desired, add an additional tablespoon of cider vinegar the last 15 minutes of cooking. Yield: about 3 cups.

Assembly

Hot dogs, grilled

Hot dog buns, steamed

Plain yellow mustard

Chopped onion

Coleslaw or sauerkraut

Alabama Coney Sauce

Place hot dogs in buns and top with mustard, onion, coleslaw or sauerkraut, and Alabama Coney Sauce. Serve immediately.

More Cool Dogs in Alabama

Dew Drop Inn

1808 Old Shell Road, Mobile, AL 36607

(251) 473-7872

Chris' Hot Dogs

138 Dexter Avenue, Montgomery, AL 36104

(334) 265-6850

Gus's Hot Dogs

1915 4th Avenue North, Birmingham, AL 35203

(205) 251-4540

Arkansas

Hot Dog Alley

2201 E Central Ave, Bentonville, AR 72712

(479) 271-6633

Bentonville, located in the northwestern tip of Arkansas, is home to Wal-Mart Stores, Inc., and Hot Dog Alley, known for its tasty dogs and a variety of toppings. All-beef hot dogs are replaced with turkey or veggie franks upon request. All the traditional toppings are available: chili, cheese, mustard, relish, and sauerkraut, and there's even a Chicago-style dog. The tasty taco dog is served up with salsa, lettuce, tomato, and cheese. Hot Dog Alley held its First Annual Hot Dog Eating Contest on May 20, 2006. Perhaps the champion will go on to compete in a future Fourth of July International Hot Dog Eating Contest at Nathan's in Coney Island.

Gone But Not Forgotten

Folks in Little Rock, Arkansas, still lament the passing of their all-time favorite hot dog eatery, Perciful's Drive-In. *The Arkansas Democrat-Gazette* has received many requests over the years for Perciful's hot dog sauce and slaw formulas. The following no-frills recipes are based on those provided by Mary Jo Lusk of Hot Springs, Arkansas. The sauce is very mild as is the slaw, which tastes mostly of mustard.

Perciful-style Hot Dogs

Perciful-style Sauce

1 1/2 pounds ground chuck
Beef broth or water
1 medium onion, chopped medium
1 (6-ounce) can tomato paste
1 tablespoon celery seed
3 teaspoons salt
4 teaspoons sugar
2 tablespoons Gebhardt's chili powder
1/4 teaspoon garlic powder
1/2 teaspoon ground black pepper
2 teaspoons ground cumin

Crumble the ground chuck into a medium-sized pot. Add beef broth (which delivers more flavor) or water just to cover the meat, and mix well with a slotted spoon in order to further break up the beef. Add remaining ingredients and bring to a boil, then lower heat and simmer for 30 minutes, stirring frequently. Yield: about 6 cups.

Perciful-style Slaw

1/2 large head cabbage
1 cup quality mayonnaise, such as Hellman's
1/2 cup plain yellow mustard, such a French's
2 teaspoons sugar
1/8 teaspoon celery salt

Using a food processor fitted with a small steel blade, finely grate the cabbage. Add remaining ingredients and blend thoroughly. Cover and keep refrigerated until ready to use. Yield: about 4 cups.

Assembly

Grilled hot dogs
Heated hot dog buns
Perciful-style Sauce
Perciful-style Slaw

Place grilled hot dogs in heated buns. Top with Perciful-style Sauce and Perciful-style Slaw to taste and serve immediately.

Delaware

Deerhead Hot Dogs

620 South Maryland Avenue, Wilmington, DE 19804

(302) 998-4191

Deerhead Hot Dogs eateries are located throughout Wilmington, Delaware. On one of his ventures outside Philadelphia, Holly Moore visited the Maryland Avenue location and pronounced the dogs as outstanding. Holly especially liked them served with the unique Greek-style secret chili sauce, which he described as "a thick slather, with a spicy kick." The hot dogs are split before grilling, and served with mustard, chopped raw onions, and the sauce. Order a double dog and you'll get two in a single bun.

Almost Deerhead Chili Dogs

This is an adaptation of a recipe that has appeared periodically in the *News Journal,* Wilmington, Delaware; fans of Deerhead Chili claim it's about as close as one can get to the real thing.

Chili

3 pounds (80 percent lean) ground beef

2 large onions, chopped

1/2 cup plus 2 tablespoons chili powder

1 1/2 tablespoons crushed red pepper flakes

1/4 teaspoon cayenne pepper, or to taste

1 (6-ounce) can tomato paste

2 (15-ounce) cans tomato sauce

2 (15-ounce) cans beef broth

1 cup plain yellow mustard

1 large onion, chopped

In a large pot, brown the ground beef and the two chopped onions, stirring frequently to ensure the beef is broken up; drain. Add remaining ingredients except the remaining chopped onion, mixing well.

Simmer over low heat for 1 hour and 45 minutes, stirring frequently. Add remaining onion to the sauce and simmer an additional 15 minutes, stirring occasionally. This chili freezes well for up to 3 months. Yield: about 12 cups.

Assembly

Hot dogs, split almost in half and grilled

Hot dog buns, toasted

Plain yellow mustard

Chili

Grated cheddar cheese (optional)

Chopped onion

Place grilled hot dogs in toasted buns and top with mustard, Chili, cheese, and onion. Serve immediately.

Florida

Hot Dog Heaven

5355 East Colonial Drive, Orlando, FL 32807

(407) 282-5746

www.hotdogheaven.com

Marked by a giant fork-speared frank that insinuates devilishly good eats, Hot Dog Heaven has graced the Orlando fast food scene since 1987. The eatery is a southern outpost of the Chicago-style hot dog, featuring Vienna Beef hot dogs, poppy seed buns, and hot sport peppers. There are even Chicago hot tamales on the menu. But there's a definite southern twist on the menu, too. The basic slaw dog comes with additional options like kraut, cheese, or chili.

Kraut & Slaw Dog

This may appear to be an unlikely combination, but the slight tartness of the coleslaw contrasts nicely with the mild, hot sauerkraut, delivering a delicious contrast in flavors.

Vinegar Slaw

1/2 large head cabbage, cored

1/2 large green bell pepper, seeded and deveined

1 small carrot, peeled

1/2 small onion

1/4 cup sugar

1/2 teaspoon salt

1/4 teaspoon mustard seed

1/2 teaspoon celery seed

1/4 teaspoon ground black pepper

3/4 cup white vinegar

Using a food processor, finely shred cabbage, bell pepper, carrot, and onion. Place the vegetables in a medium bowl and mix well.

In a small bowl, combine sugar, salt, mustard seeds, celery seeds, and pepper and stir in the vinegar. Pour vinegar mixture over vegetables and mix well. Cover and refrigerate for at least 1 hour to allow flavors to blend. Yield: about 4 cups.

Assembly

Vienna Beef hot dogs (or substitute hot dog of choice), steamed or charbroiled

Poppy seed buns, toasted

Sauerkraut, heated (see page 38)

Vinegar Slaw

Plain yellow mustard

Place hot dogs in toasted buns and top with Sauerkraut, Vinegar Slaw, and mustard. Serve immediately.

Georgia

Dinglewood Pharmacy

1939 Wynnton Road, Columbus, GA 31906

(706) 322-0616

The Dinglewood Pharmacy, which opened for business in 1918, was destined to become legendary throughout Georgia. It's the home of the original scrambled dog served at the Dinglewood's lunch counter. For more than forty years, until his retirement in 2002, Lieutenant Charles Stevens made the scrambled dog and the special secret chili that tops it. Born the day after Veterans Day, Stevens's parents named him in honor of the military; Lieutenant is his first name, not a military rank. Stevens always pointed out that he was not the creator of the scrambled dog; credit for that goes to a man named Henry "Sport" Brown who died in the 1950s, but it was Stevens who kept the tradition alive, and most folks in Columbus claim he perfected the dish. The Dinglewood scrambled dog is a hot dog that is split in half and placed on an open bun that rests in a banana split dish. It's then smothered with Lieutenant's secret chili (still made at Dinglewood) and an impressive array of toppings.

Dinglewood-style Scrambled Dog

Hot dog buns, toasted
Hot dogs, boiled and split in half
Plain yellow mustard
Ketchup
1/2 cup chili
American cheese, 1 slice per hot dog (optional)
Chopped onions
Dill pickle slices
Oyster crackers

Place open bun in a banana split dish or on a large plate, and add the hot dog. Top with mustard, ketchup, chili, cheese, onions, pickles, and oyster crackers. Serve immediately.

4-Way Lunch

Corner of East Main and South Gilmer Streets, Cartersville, GA 31021

No phone

The tantalizing smell of onion gravy wafts daily from a little red diner in Cartersville, Georgia, enticing passersby, locals and strangers alike, with its promise of good eats. This is the famous 4-Way Lunch, operated by the Garrison family since 1930. Sold to new owners in 2004, it's still known for great hot dogs and hamburgers, usually loaded with chili, accompanied by fries topped with delicious onion gravy, and for the sign behind the counter that says, "This isn't Burger King. You don't get it your way. You get it our way, or you don't get the damn thing."

Fries with Onion Gravy

Onion Gravy

1/4 cup vegetable oil
4 medium onions, chopped
1 tablespoon flour
1 (14-ounce) can beef broth
Pepper to taste

Heat oil in a 12-inch frying pan over medium heat and add the onions. Cook slowly over medium-low heat, stirring occasionally, until onions are deep golden brown, being careful not to burn the onions toward the end of the cooking time. Stir in the flour, add 1/2 cup beef broth, and stir well. Cook, stirring, over medium-low heat for 3 minutes; add 1/2 cup more beef broth, mixing well, and continue to cook, stirring occasionally, for 10 minutes. Add remaining broth, mix well, and cook 5 minutes longer. Season the gravy with pepper. Yield: about 1 1/2 cups.

Assembly

2 cups grated cheddar cheese (optional)
1 pound french fries, cooked crispy
Salt and pepper to taste
1 1/2 cups Onion Gravy

If using cheese, preheat the broiler. Place cooked fries on a rimmed baking sheet and sprinkle with salt and pepper. Sprinkle cheese evenly over the fries and place under the broiler just until cheese melts. Remove from broiler, place fries on a serving platter, and pour the Onion Gravy over the top. Serves 4 to 6.

Nu-Way Weiners

430 Cotton Avenue, Macon, GA 31201

(478) 743-1366

www.nu-wayweiners.com

Nu-Way Weiners has grown and flourished over the years, and the business now encompasses many other locations in central Georgia, but the place to go is the original site at 430 Cotton in Macon. Longtime patrons say it has barely changed since Greek immigrant James Mallis opened his storefront in 1916. Having passed through New York, Mallis noted the American craze for hot dogs, and it became the inspiration for his own business when he moved on to Macon. Nu-Way says the secret to their bright red, private-label pork-and-beef "weiners" is the fact that they are grilled, not boiled. Nu-Way weiners are served in steamed buns with a choice of toppings such as their secret chili and barbecue sauces, fresh homemade creamy sweet slaw, cheese, mustard, and onions.

Southern Barbecue–Sweet Slaw Dogs

This creamy sweet slaw is perfect as a topping for hot dogs. The recipe is reprinted with permission from *Deep South Staples* by Chef Robert St. John.

Sweet Slaw

1 cup sugar

1 cup mayonnaise

1/2 cup white vinegar

2 tablespoons milk

2 tablespoons prepared yellow mustard, such as French's

1/8 teaspoon salt

1/2 teaspoon celery seeds

6 to 8 peppercorns or 1/2 teaspoon ground black pepper

6 cups finely shredded cabbage

2 cups finely shredded carrots

Process all ingredients except cabbage and carrots in a blender or food processor until smooth. Toss dressing with cabbage and carrots. Yield: about 8 cups.

Assembly

Pork-and-beef hot dogs, grilled

Hot dog buns, toasted

Barbecue sauce, tomato-based

Sweet Slaw

Place grilled hot dogs in toasted buns. Top with a slathering of your favorite barbecue sauce and a generous helping of Sweet Slaw. Serve immediately.

The Varsity Drive-In

61 North Avenue NW, Atlanta, GA 30308

(404) 881-1706

www.thevarsity.com

In 1928, Frank Gordy moved his restaurant, the Yellow Jacket, to its present location, renamed it the Varsity, and launched what would become the "World's Largest Drive-In." There is drive-in curb service as well as indoor eating. The Varsity's size alone can be intimidating to first-time patrons, but so can the jargon and the counter staff where speed is the key to serving two miles of hot dogs and a ton and a half of potatoes to some 17,000 customers daily. Pay attention to the warning, "Have your money in your hand and your order in your mind." It's soon followed by the rapid-fire question, "What'll ya have, what'll ya have?"—and you'd better be ready. The Varsity makes its own pimiento cheese with cheddar imported from England; a pimiento cheese/slaw dog is a southern favorite and a true taste of the South.

Pimiento Cheese Dogs

Pimiento Cheese

10-ounces quality sharp cheddar cheese, grated

1 (4-ounce) jar pimientos, drained

1/2 cup quality mayonnaise, such as Hellman's

1 tablespoon lemon juice

1 teaspoon Worcestershire sauce

1/8 teaspoon cayenne pepper, or more to taste

In a mixing bowl, combine all ingredients. Mix well with a fork, mashing the mixture a bit to create a chunky-style spread.

Store in a tightly covered container, and refrigerate for several hours or overnight, allowing flavors to blend. Yield: 2 cups.

Assembly

Beef-and-pork hot dogs, grilled

Hot dog buns, toasted

2 tablespoons Pimiento Cheese per hot dog, or to taste

Place grilled hot dogs in toasted buns. Top with Pimiento Cheese and serve immediately.

Kentucky

Dixie Chili

2421 Madison Avenue, Covington, KY 41014

(859) 431-7444

www.dixiechili.com

Covington's proximity to Cincinnati places it directly in the middle of the Cincy chili wars and endless arguments over who serves the best of the local, definitely Greek-style chili that comes atop both spaghetti and hot dogs. In Covington, Dixie Chili claims to be Northern Kentucky's very first chili parlor. Nicholas D. Sarakatsannis established Dixie in 1929 after a brief stint working at the Empress Chili parlor in Cincinnati; the first location was in Newport, Kentucky, and Sarakatsannis served his own rendition of Cincinnati-style chili. The business thrived and today the family operates several restaurants in the area. "Papa Nick's" secret recipe, based on lean beef chuck or loin combined with Bermuda onions, fresh garlic, and a secret blend of spices, is made fresh daily and served atop spaghetti in the usual five variations: spaghetti, chili, beans, onions, and grated cheddar cheese. However, Dixie took the concept a step farther and added a six-way version by including chopped garlic as an option. Their Coneys also call for Dixie chili: steamed wieners placed in steamed buns are first flavored with a squirt of mustard, followed by a covering of spicy chili, chopped onions, and an optional dose of grated cheddar cheese. Dixie offers a tasty variation called the "Alligator" and a chili-cheese sandwich devoid of the wiener.

Dixie-style "Alligator" Wiener

Hot dogs, steamed

Hot dog buns, steamed

2 tablespoons grated cheddar cheese per dog

Plain yellow mustard, to taste

Mayonnaise, to taste

1 dill pickle spear per dog

Place steamed hot dogs in the steamed buns. Top each with cheddar cheese, mustard, mayonnaise, and a dill pickle spear. Serve immediately.

Sources: Dixie Chili can be purchased at any of the Dixie restaurants or via mail order on their website www.dixiechili.com.

Louisiana

Arnaud's Remoulade

309 Bourbon Street, New Orleans, LA 70112

(504) 523-0377

www.remoulade.com

The classiest, if not the most eclectic, hot dog in New Orleans is found at Arnaud's Remoulade, a casual eatery that's an offshoot of the legendary French Quarter restaurant established in 1918. Arnaud's remoulade dog, a grilled all-beef frank topped with Creole remoulade sauce, is a tasty treat popular with visitors and locals alike.

New Orleans Remoulade Dog

This is an adaptation of a recipe from *Too Good To Be True* by the late Chet Beckwith of Baton Rouge, Louisiana. It's one of the best versions to be found. You'll want to serve it with tossed salads too.

Remoulade Sauce

1 cup quality mayonnaise, such as Hellman's

1/2 cup ketchup

1/2 cup thinly sliced green onions, tops and bottoms

1/2 cup finely chopped celery

1/2 medium green bell pepper, seeded and thinly diced

1/2 medium onion, finely chopped

1/2 cup horseradish

1 1/2 tablespoons lemon juice

1 1/2 tablespoons Worcestershire sauce

1 1/2 teaspoons dried basil

1 bay leaf

1/4 cup cider vinegar

1 large clove garlic, finely minced

1 1/2 tablespoons Tabasco sauce

Salt and pepper, to taste

Mix all ingredients well and store in the refrigerator. It will keep for a week to ten days. Serve over hot dogs, boiled shrimp, or a lettuce salad. Yield: 1 quart.

Assembly

All-beef hot dogs, grilled

Hot dog buns, toasted

2 tablespoons Remoulade Sauce per hot dog, or to taste

Place grilled hot dogs in the toasted buns and top with Remoulade Sauce. Serve immediately.

Cajun Fries

Sprinkle hot, crispy french fries with Creole seasoning, such as Tony Chachere's, to taste and serve immediately. Most commercial versions of Creole seasoning are relatively salty so use caution. Source: Tony Chachere's Original Creole Seasoning, as well as a salt-free version, are available at most supermarkets or it may be ordered at www.tonychachere.com.

More Cool Dogs in Louisiana

Lucky Dogs (Corporate Headquarters)

517 Gravier Street, New Orleans, LA 70130

(504) 523-9260

Domilise's Sandwich Shop and Bar

5240 Annunication Street, New Orleans, LA 70115

(504) 899-9126

Maryland

Ann's Dari-Creme

7918 Ritchie Highway, Glen Burnie, MD 21061

(410) 761-1231

Folks in Maryland often like their hot dogs split and deep-fried, a process that has earned the name "frizzled dogs." At Ann's Dari-Creme, they use foot-long wonders that are served in sub rolls topped with chili, onions, mustard, and cheese. Terrific ice cream and shakes have contributed to the popularity of this favorite fast food eatery. Ann's has been in business since 1953.

Curtis' Coney Island Famous Weiners

35 North Liberty Street, Cumberland, MD 21502

(301) 777-0380

In Cumberland, located in Western Maryland, Curtis' Coney Island Famous Weiners is a local legend, and you can't miss the eatery—eleven different hand-painted signs mark the place. The original business was Curtis' confectionary shop, established in 1905. In 1918, weiners were added to the menu and served with a thin, mild chili sauce. Louis Giatras, whose father was a Greek immigrant who worked at the confectionary store, bought the business in the 1950s along with the  secret recipe for the Coney Island chili sauce. Every day, 365 days a year, a member of the Giatras family arrives at 4:00 AM to prepare the secret sauce behind locked doors, and as business begins, the delicious smell of that "Original Coney Island Sauce" draws customers in like a magnet. The grilled hot dogs are cooked to each customer's desired degree of doneness, then served topped with the Giatras's chili meat sauce, chopped onion, and brown mustard.

Maryland-style Coney Island Hot Dogs

Coney Island Sauce

1 pound (80 percent lean) ground beef

1 cup beef broth

1 large onion, chopped

1/3 cup apple cider vinegar

5 ounces tomato puree

1 tablespoon plus 1 teaspoon quality chili powder

1 teaspoon salt

2 teaspoons celery seed

1 teaspoon ground black pepper

In a medium saucepan, combine beef and broth and mix well with a slotted spoon to break up the beef. Add remaining ingredients and mix well.

Simmer the mixture, uncovered, over medium-low heat, stirring frequently, for 2 hours or until thickened. Yield: about 2 1/2 cups.

Assembly

Hot dogs, grilled

Hot dog buns, steamed or toasted

Coney Island Sauce

Chopped onion

Brown mustard, such as Gulden's

Place hot dogs in buns and top with Coney Island Sauce, onion, and mustard. Serve immediately.

Mississippi

Hot dogs in Mississippi tend to come in two forms: chili cheese dogs and corn dogs. Mississippi's homegrown Bumpers Drive-In, with some thirty locations throughout the state, offers both kinds of dogs along with those fried pickles so beloved by folks in the South. Bumpers also serves really great Cajun fries, topped with melted Swiss and American cheese and bacon and served with ranch dressing.

Mississippi Cajun Fries

1 pound hot french fries, cooked crispy
Louisiana Original Cajun Seasoning, to taste
1 cup grated Swiss cheese
3 slices American cheese, cut into 1-inch squares
4 slices bacon, fried crisp, drained, and crumbled
1 cup Hidden Valley Original Ranch Dressing, or to taste

Preheat broiler. Place hot fries on a rimmed baking sheet and sprinkle lightly with Cajun seasoning. Top with cheeses and broil until the cheese is hot and melted.

Remove from broiler, transfer fries to a platter, and sprinkle with the crumbled bacon. Serve immediately with the ranch dressing for dipping. Serves 4.

Source: Louisiana Original Cajun Seasoning may be ordered from:

www.livecrawfish.com
22195 Talbot Drive
Plaquemine, LA 70764
(866) LA-CFOOD

Mississippi's Southern Sides: Fried Dill Pickles and Comeback Sauce

Fried dill pickles are a specialty of the Deep South and are said to have originated at the Hollywood Café in Robinsonville, Mississippi. Having run out of catfish, a cook dunked dill pickle chips in the fish batter, fried them up in hot oil, and served them to hungry patrons who proceeded to anoint the creator with high praise. An opposing story, recorded by John T. Edge in *Southern Belly,* claims they were invented in Atkins, Arkansas, at the Duchess Drive In. Experts and devotees claim they should always be made with dill pickle chips, never spears. Some eateries serve them with ranch dressing while others serve them with Mississippi's equally famous Comeback Sauce.

Fried Dill Pickles

1/3 cup cornmeal
3/4 cup all-purpose flour
1/2 teaspoon garlic powder
1/8 teaspoon salt
1/2 teaspoon paprika
1 teaspoon ground cayenne pepper
1 egg, lightly beaten
1/3 cup pickle juice
1/2 teaspoon Frank's Red Hot Sauce
1 tablespoon flour
2 pints sliced dill pickles
Canola oil for deep-frying
Comeback Sauce (below) or ranch dressing

In a bowl, combine cornmeal, 3/4 cup flour, garlic powder, salt, paprika, and cayenne pepper, mixing well; set aside. In another bowl, whisk the egg, pickle juice, hot sauce, and 1 tablespoon flour; set aside. Drain the pickles well between paper towels. In a deep frying pan or pot, heat the oil to 375 degrees. Dip pickles in egg mixture, then in the cornmeal mixture and deep-fry, a few at a time, until golden brown, about 1 to 2 minutes. Drain on paper towels and serve hot. Serve with Comeback Sauce or ranch dressing for dipping. Yield: about 48 pickles.

Note: If desired, reduce the cayenne pepper and the hot sauce to tone down the spiciness.

Rotisserie Comeback Sauce

This recipe is adapted from one credited to the now defunct Rotisserie Restaurant in Jackson, Mississippi.

1/4 cup chopped onion
1 cup quality mayonnaise, such as Hellman's
2 cloves garlic, chopped
1/4 cup prepared chili sauce, such as Heinz
1 tablespoon prepared plain yellow mustard
1 tablespoon Worcestershire sauce
1 teaspoon black pepper
1 teaspoon hot pepper sauce, such as Tabasco or Frank's
    Red Hot Sauce, or more, to taste
1/2 cup quality vegetable oil

Combine all ingredients except oil in a food processor and pulse to combine. With processor running, slowly add the oil until completely incorporated and mixture is emulsified. Place sauce in a bowl, cover, and refrigerate for at least 2 hours before serving. Use as a dipping sauce for french fries or as a topping on hot dogs. Yield: 1 3/4 cups.

North Carolina

As Greek immigrants headed south, many established hot dog eateries in North Carolina. Today, many of the old restaurants are long gone, and other hot dog emporiums have sprung up in their place. Chili dogs are very popular, but one must remember that this is barbecue country where coleslaw is frequently served, so it's only natural that North Carolinians added slaw to their hot dogs. In North Carolina's Piedmont area around Lexington, red slaw prevails; heavily flavored with vinegar, it's tinted red with the addition of ketchup. In eastern North Carolina, yellow slaw, gussied up with mustard, rules.

Buzzy and Bear's Grill

9709-B Sam Furr Road, Huntersville, NC 28078

(704) 895-2692

www.buzzyandbearsgrill.com

Buzzy and Bear's Grill is a relative newcomer to the North Carolina hot dog scene, but the owners' emphasis on quality and service takes no backseat. This business is really a love story. Lisa (Buzzy) and Peter (Bear) Fleck, who were high school sweethearts in 1956, were reintroduced by mutual friends in 1998 and married a year later. Relocation to the Carolinas found them craving the taste of flame-broiled hot dogs, so they decided to make good use of their lifelong love of food and cooking, and Buzzy and Bear's was the delicious result. Jumbo-sized all-beef "pushcart-style" dogs are flame-broiled and served on locally baked fresh buns that are griddle toasted with their signature "butter and spice sauce," then garnished with savory selections that include freshly made chili, slaw, and white wine sauerkraut. The slaw is vinegar-laced, lending an added snap to the dogs.

Piedmont-style North Carolina Dogs and Coleslaw

This delicious tangy, red, Piedmont-style coleslaw recipe is reprinted with permission from Bob Garner's *North Carolina Barbecue: Flavored by Time,* John F. Blair, Publisher.

Peidmont-style Coleslaw

1 medium-size, firm head cabbage

1/2 cup apple cider vinegar

1/2 cup sugar

2/3 cup ketchup

2 teaspoons salt

2 teaspoons black pepper

2 teaspoons Texas Pete hot sauce

Keep cabbage refrigerated until ready to use. Remove outer leaves and core from cabbage. Cut head in half and grate, using a food processor or hand grater. Return cabbage to refrigerator. In a small mixing bowl, combine vinegar, sugar, ketchup, and seasonings. Mix until well blended. Remove cabbage from refrigerator and pour mixture over it. Mix with a large spoon until well blended.

Note: This may look dry at first, but there's plenty of liquidto moisten the cabbage thoroughly if you'll keep mixing. Refrigerate 1 hour before serving. Serves 20.

Assembly

Beef-and-pork hot dogs, grilled

Hot dog buns, toasted

Coney Island–style Sauce (such as New York System Hot Wiener Sauce on page 55 or Aiken Pool Hall Chili on page 79)

Plain yellow mustard

Freshly chopped onions

Piedmont-style Coleslaw

Place grilled hot dogs in toasted buns. Top with Coney Island–style Sauce, mustard, chopped onions, and Piedmont-style Coleslaw. Serve immediately.

Jay Bee's

320 Mocksville Highway, Statesville, NC 28625

(704) 872-8033

Jay Bee's is located in Statesville, the next fair-sized city north of Charlotte, and the eatery is identified by a welcome sign that also warns, "This ain't no fast food joint!" Established in 1981, the eatery offers both drive-through service and in-house dining. Jay Bee's is noted for its all-beef or pork-and-beef foot-long hot dogs "All the Way," which means yellow mustard, onions, spicy slaw, and chili. An old favorite is the foot-long Prairie Dog slathered with mahogany-hued barbecue sauce, melted cheddar cheese, and chopped onions.

North Carolina Barbecue Dog

Hot dogs, grilled
Hot dog buns, steamed
Prepared tomato-based barbecue sauce, such as
     KC Masterpiece Hickory Brown Sugar, to taste
2 tablespoons cheddar cheese per dog, melted
Chopped onion, to taste

Place grilled hot dogs in the steamed buns and drizzle with barbecue sauce to taste. Top with melted cheddar and chopped onion and serve immediately.

Eastern North Carolina Coleslaw

This coleslaw is outstanding on hot dogs. The recipe is reprinted with permission from Bob Garner's *North Carolina Barbecue: Flavored by Time,* John F. Blair, Publisher.

1 medium-size, firm head cabbage
1 1/2 cups mayonnaise
1/3 cup plain yellow mustard
3/4 cup sweet pickle cubes
2 tablespoons apple cider vinegar
1/2 cup sugar
1 tablespoon celery seed
1 1/2 teaspoons salt
1/8 teaspoon black pepper

Keep cabbage refrigerated until ready to use, and do not allow it to reach room temperature once you begin. Remove outer leaves and core from cabbage. Cut head in half and grate fine, using a food processor or hand grater. In a large bowl, combine cabbage, mayonnaise, mustard, sweet pickle cubes, vinegar, sugar, and seasonings. Mix thoroughly and chill for 1 hour before serving. Serves 20.

South Carolina

City Billiards

208 Richland Avenue West, Aiken, SC 29801

(803) 649-7362

www.aiken-explorer.com/ad-city-billiards.htm

City Billiards doesn't get a whole lot of press, but perusing Internet postings on where to find a great hot dog inevitably leads to comments about "the Aiken pool hall's famous chili dogs." City Billiards is located adjacent to the Alley, once a row of blacksmith shops and stables now renovated into restaurants and shops, in historic downtown Aiken. Given the fact that South Carolinians favor mustard-based barbecue sauce, it's not surprising they favor a chili that's fairly heavy on the mustard, too.

"Aiken Pool Hall" Chili Dogs

This is an adaptation of a recipe that many fans claim produces a sweet, mild chili similar to that served at City Billiards for over fifty years.

Chili

1 pound (80 percent lean) ground beef
Cold water
2 large onions, chopped
1/4 cup plain yellow mustard
1 tablespoon sugar
2 teaspoons chili powder
2 teaspoons apple cider vinegar
1 cup ketchup
Salt, to taste

Crumble ground beef into a 4-quart pot. Add just enough water to make a thick mixture, and stir until smooth.

Add remaining ingredients and mix well. Cook, uncovered, over medium-low heat for at least 1 hour, adding a bit more water if needed, until thick. Add salt to taste. Yield: about 5 cups.

Assembly

Hot dogs, boiled or grilled
Hot dog buns, steamed or toasted
Chili
Chopped onion

Place hot dogs in buns. Top with Chili and onion and serve immediately.

Tennessee

St. Elmo Dog House

3914 St. Elmo Avenue, Chattanooga, TN 37409

(423) 821-1717

Marked by bright red double doors, the St. Elmo Dog House is one cool place. They specialize in hot dogs and the menu reflects a definite creativity that's hard to resist. Tennessee is known for its cornbread so one naturally expects corn dogs at a great weenie eatery and sure enough, the Dog House offers two choices made with either regular-sized beef or veggie dogs: the "Waffle Dogger Classic," made with homemade batter and served with mustard, ketchup, or hot sauce for dipping, and the "Waffle Dogger Primo," made with a Mexican cornbread batter. There's a good roster of regular dogs that includes chili, slaw, and kraut, but one is well advised to be more adventuresome. The "T.C.B." comes with tomato, cheese, and bacon adorned with a drizzle of barbecue sauce. And then there's the luscious "Pam's Pizza Dog," a clever variation that adds an Italian twist to the all-American frank. Southern touches to the menu include such niceties as deviled eggs, potato salad, or a side of slaw.

Pizza Dogs

These yummy hot dogs are the perfect solution for those who crave both pups and pizza!

Beef-and-pork hot dogs, grilled or charbroiled
Hot dog buns, toasted
1/4 cup grated whole-milk mozzarella cheese per bun
Hot or mild pepper rings, drained (optional)
6 pieces thinly sliced pepperoni per bun
2 tablespoons warm marinara sauce per bun

While the hot dogs are cooking, toast the buns and preheat the broiler. Just before the hot dogs are done, sprinkle cheese on the toasted buns and top with pepper rings and pepperoni. Place under broiler for 3 to 5 minutes, or until cheese is melted and bubbly. Remove from broiler, place a dog on each roll, and top with marinara sauce. Serve immediately.

Virginia

Anyone looking for great hot dogs in Virginia is well advised to head straight for Roanoke. There you'll find two of the oldest restaurants in the city. They've both survived the continued encroachment of fast food chains simply because they are run by friendly people who care about their customers and who believe in serving quality food.

Roanoke Weiner Stand

25 Campbell Avenue SE, Roanoke, VA 24011

(540) 342-6932

The Roanoke Weiner Stand, founded in 1916, has a long heritage of Greek ownership. The landmark eatery is located on the corner of Campbell Avenue and Market Square, home of Roanoke's historic farmers market, which was established in 1884, the oldest such continuously operating city market in Virginia. The countermen at the Roanoke Weiner Stand remember the days when mountain farmers came to the market and breakfasted on Weiner Stand hot dogs at dawn. The wieners are grilled, the buns are steamed, and the majority of customers are enticed by the smell of the establishment's secret-recipe chili. An order for "One With" results in a dog topped with mustard, onions, and chili. No one minds standing while they eat—it's a great opportunity to study the many photos on the wall that recount Roanoke's history.

The Texas Tavern

114 West Church Avenue, Roanoke, VA 24011

(540) 342-4825

www.texastavern-inc.com

The white brick Texas Tavern isn't a tavern at all—no alcoholic beverages are sold—but it's famous for grilled hot dogs, Texas Tavern Relish, and Texas Tavern Chile, and it's another Roanoke landmark. Isaac N. (Nick) Bullington, onetime advance man for the Ringling Brothers Circus, founded it in 1930. Bullington had acquired a recipe for chile from a San Antonio, Texas, hotel

chef that he used for hot dogs. Today, James Matthew Bullington, great-grandson of the founder, runs the eatery, and it's still referred to as "Roanoke's Millionaire's Club" because every customer is treated like a millionaire. The chile contains a proprietary combination of meat, beans, and spices, and it's sold at the tavern in pints, quarts, and gallons for those who need to nurse their cravings from afar. Although Texans decry the use of beans in "real chili," patrons of the Texas Tavern think they're just fine.

Texas Chuck Wagon Chili Dogs

This is not the Texas Tavern's secret chili recipe, but it does make a fantastic topping for hot dogs, producing a truly pedigreed pooch.

Chili

1/2 pound dried pinto beans
2 (14-ounce) cans beef broth, divided
1 1/2 pounds (90 percent lean) ground beef
1 1/2 tablespoons butter
1 medium onion, chopped
2 cloves garlic, peeled and chopped
1 (6-ounce) can tomato paste
1/4 cup quality chili powder
1 teaspoon salt
1/2 cup water
1 (15-ounce) can crushed tomatoes in puree
1/2 teaspoon ground marjoram
3/4 teaspoon crushed red pepper flakes
1/4 teaspoon cayenne pepper

Wash and pick over beans, put in a bowl and soak in water overnight. Next day, drain and rinse the beans and put them in a pot with 1 1/2 cans of the beef broth. Bring to a boil, lower heat, and simmer the beans for 1 hour.

In a medium pot, brown the ground beef and drain off all fat. Melt the butter in a medium frying pan and sauté the onion over low heat until it's soft and transparent. Add the garlic and sauté for 1 minute. Add the onion mixture and all remaining ingredients to the pot with the beef and mix well. Simmer the chili over low heat, partially covered and stirring occasionally, for 3 hours or until beans are tender and the flavors are melded. If the mixture becomes too thick, add a bit more water. This chili freezes well for up to 3 months. Yield: about 7 cups.

Assembly

Hot dogs, grilled
Hot dog buns, toasted
Chili
Grated cheddar cheese
Chopped onion

Place hot dogs in buns and top with Chili, cheese, and onion. Serve immediately.

Washington, D.C.

Ben's Chili Bowl

1213 U Street N.W., Washington, DC 20009

(202) 667-0909

www.benschilibowl.com

Washington D.C.'s Shaw neighborhood is less than a mile from the White House. Duke Ellington was born there, and for years it was the cultural capital of black America, attracting jazz greats like Ella Fitzgerald and Louis Armstrong. Because of its large number of theaters, the area was referred to as "Black Broadway." Shaw has recently been revitalized—the Lincoln Theater and other landmarks have been renovated, and there are loads of shops and restaurants attracting tourists and locals alike. But there's one landmark that has barely changed since it was founded by Ben and Virginia Ali in 1958—Ben's Chili Bowl, a local institution and national treasure.

Now under the direction of sons Nizam and Kamal Ali, Ben's is the home of Washington, D.C.'s signature dish, the Half-Smoke—a chubby, quarter-pound, spicy beef-and-pork sausage that's lightly smoked, similar to smoked Polish sausage. Kamal Ali says that his father, Ben Ali, was the first in the area to adapt what was originally a breakfast sausage as a luncheon sandwich. The elder Mr. Ali was from Trinidad, and accustomed to spicy food, so he decided to jazz things up by also serving spicy hot chili at his restaurant. Ben's serves three versions of chili: a spicy, thin meat sauce served on hot dogs; regular chili; and a vegetarian chili. Each version incorporates the spicy blend of chili powder specially formulated for the restaurant, and the recipes themselves have barely changed since Mr. Ali developed them almost fifty years ago.

At Ben's Chili Bowl, "Home of the Famous Chili Dog," the half-smoke is split and grilled, then served on a steamed bun topped with mustard, onions, and Ben's proprietary hot dog sauce. A diverse clientele sprinkled with plenty of celebrities is attracted as much by the food as by the trappings of the diner where the décor is marked by a Formica counter, red plastic-covered barstools, and a jukebox playing familiar tunes.

D.C. Half-Smokes with Ben's-style Chili

The hot dog sauce at Ben's Chili Bowl is a closely guarded secret, but this recipe, adapted from a formula for their spicy chili provided by Mrs. Ali to *Essence* magazine (without Ben's secret spice mixture), delivers a tantalizing taste of Washington's famous hot dog emporium.

Ben's Chili

1 pound (90 percent lean) ground beef

1 tablespoon vegetable oil

3/4 cup chopped onion

1/4 cup chopped green bell pepper

1 large garlic clove, finely chopped

1 (14.5-ounce) can stewed tomatoes with juice

1 1/2 tablespoons tomato sauce

1 1/2 cups beef broth

3 tablespoons quality chili powder

1/2 teaspoon ground cumin seed

3/4 teaspoon salt

1/4 teaspoon cayenne pepper

1/4 teaspoon crushed red pepper

1 (16-ounce) can kidney beans, drained and rinsed

In a heavy, medium pot, sauté ground beef over medium high heat, stirring with a slotted spoon to break it up; drain off all fat, transfer beef to a bowl, and set aside. Add the oil to the pot and sauté the onion and bell pepper over low heat, stirring frequently, just until the vegetables begin to soften.

Add the garlic the last minute of cooking. Return the beef to the pot along with all remaining ingredients except the kidney beans. Mix well and cook over low heat, stirring frequently, for 1 hour. Add the kidney beans and cook for an additional 15 minutes. Yield: about 4 1/2 cups.

Assembly

Half-smokes, split and grilled

Steamed buns

Ben's Chili

Plain yellow mustard

Freshly chopped onion

Place half-smokes in steamed buns and top with Ben's Chili, mustard, and onion. Serve immediately.

Sources: Ben's Chili Bowl serves half-smokes manufactured by Manger Packing, Inc. Manger will ship its half-smokes, as well as many other brands of sausages and hot dogs. Orders require a minimum ten-pound purchase.

Manger Packing, Inc.
125 South Franklintown Road
Baltimore, MD 21223
(410) 233-0126

West Virginia

If busy West Virginians aren't noshing on pepperoni rolls, they're headed for the nearest hot dog restaurant. Hot dogs, served with various secret specialty sauces, have achieved a noble status in the state. Close proximity to Ohio and Kentucky may account for the prevalence of hot dog sauces, with undertones of cinnamon, that bear a serious resemblance to Cincinnati chili. In the Huntington area, it's called chili, but in the Fairmont area of North Central West Virginia, home of hot dog eateries like Lupo's Lunch and Yann's Hot Dog Stand, it's called hot dog sauce.

Stewart's Original Hot Dogs

2445 5th Avenue, Huntington, WV 25703

(304) 529-4700

www.stewartshotdogs.com

John and Gertrude Mandt established Stewart's back in 1932, selling only root beer and popcorn, but it wasn't long before hot dogs, topped with Gertrude's own chili sauce, were added to the menu. Stewart's is still family-owned and now includes several locations, including the original bright orange drive-in on 5th Avenue in Huntington. The specialty, of course, is a frank served on a steamed bun topped with Stewart's secret chili sauce, mustard, and onion. Other options  include slaw dogs as well as a chili bun that excludes the frank. Today, Stewart's ships its hot dogs and all the trimmings around the country, and shipments have even been sent to American troops in the Middle East.

West Virginia–style Hot Dogs

In the Fairmont area of West Virginia, folks like their hot dog sauce with a bit of a kick; adjust the amount of hot red pepper flakes to your personal taste.

Chili Sauce

1 tablespoon olive oil

1 large onion, chopped

2 1/2 pounds (80 percent lean) ground beef

3 cups beef broth

1 (15-ounce) can tomato sauce

1 cup ketchup

1/4 cup tomato paste

2 teaspoons black pepper

2 teaspoons salt

2 tablespoons quality chili powder

2 tablespoons crushed red pepper flakes, or to taste

1/4 teaspoon ground cumin

Dash of hot red pepper sauce

In a medium pot, heat the olive oil and sauté the onion just until it starts to soften, about 5 minutes. Crumble the ground beef into the pot and add the beef broth. Stir the mixture with a slotted spoon to break up the ground beef. Add the remaining ingredients, and, over medium heat, bring just to a boil, stirring frequently with a slotted spoon to keep the beef broken up. Adjust heat to medium-low and cook, uncovered, for 2 1/2 hours, stirring occasionally, until mixture is medium-thick. The chili may be frozen for up to three months. Yield: about 7 cups.

Assembly

Hot dogs, grilled

Hot dog buns, steamed

Plain yellow mustard

Chili Sauce

Chopped onion

Placed grilled hot dogs in steamed buns. Top with mustard, Chili Sauce, and chopped onion and serve immediately.

CHAPTER 4

Hot Dogs of the Midwest: Coneys, Chicago-style Hot Dogs, and Pronto Pups

Famed Chicago Dogs are available on about every corner of the windy city. Just look for the signs and listen for the arguments.

Midwesterners enjoy a wide variety of hot dogs and toppings. Chicagoans, refusing to take a back seat to the Northeast, loudly proclaim the Chicago-style dog as our nation's finest. In Cincinnati, Ohio, fans want their franks topped with a healthy serving of the Greek-style chili unique to that area. In Michigan, Greek-influenced Coney sauces, characterized as either "wet" or "dry," overrule the famous Cincy-style chili. Fans of M*A*S*H make the trek to Tony Packo's in Toledo, Ohio, where they pay homage to a Hungarian hot dog topped with a distinctive Hungarian sauce. In Wisconsin, it's all about butter-drenched bratwurst sandwiches. And throughout the Midwest, pronto pups and corn dogs are favorite treats.

Illinois

Chicago-style Hot Dogs

Chicago has a major influence on favored foods of the Midwest. It's the home of deep dish–style pizza and the Italian beef sandwich. It's also the home of the famous frank known as the Chicago-style hot dog. Based on a Vienna all-beef frank, this distinguished dog is typically steamed (some restaurants grill or charbroil them) and served in a warm poppy seed bun topped with mustard, sweet pickle relish, chopped onion, tomato wedges or slices, sport peppers, and a dill pickle spear, then finished off with a dash of celery salt. Like New Yorkers, Chicagoans disdain ketchup, deeming it an unacceptable condiment on their franks. Today, the Chicago manner of dressing a hot dog is usually called "the works," but it's sometimes referred to as "dragging it through the garden."

Chicagoans boast of hot dog and Italian beef sandwich stands on nearly every corner, and fierce debate rages among locals and visitors alike as to where one may enjoy the best of the best. The following are some of the most popular places to enjoy a Chicago-style hot dog; note that many of these eateries have more than one location and some will ship their products.

Byron's Hot Dog Haus

1017 West Irving Park Road, Chicago, IL 60613

(773) 281-7474

The original location for one of Chicago's most legendary hot dog stands, famous for its "five napkin" Chicago-style hot dog.

Fluky's

6821 N. Western Avenue, Chicago, IL 60645

(773) 274-3652

www.flukys.com

Another "Windy City" institution, Fluky's has been selling Chicago-style hot dogs since 1929. They also claim to have developed the fluorescent green relish that appeared in the 1970s.

Gene & Jude's Red Hot Stand

2720 N. River Road, River Grove, IL 60171

(708) 452-7634

Gene & Jude's has been a favorite dog-house for Chicago suburbanites since 1946. Their unique Chicago-style dog comes on a plain bun (no poppy seeds) topped only with mustard, onion, relish, and a sport pepper—the dogs are small so most people order a double.

Gold Coast Dogs

159 N. Wabash Avenue, Chicago, IL 60601

(312) 917-1677

Gold Coast gives a twist to the traditional Chicago dog by chargrilling instead of steaming them, delivering up a crunchy yet moist and delicious result.

Poochie's

3832 Dempster Street, Skokie, IL 60076

(847) 673-0100

A no-frills eatery that garners a great deal of sentimental affection from locals, Poochie's serves a chargrilled version of the standard Chicago dog.

Portillo's Hot Dogs

100 W. Ontario Street, Chicago, IL 60610

(312) 587-8910

www.portillos.com

Portillo's epitomizes the glitzy version of Chicago's hot dog tradition, and it's the perfect place for customers who might be just a bit too squeamish to enter the doors of a typical hot dog eatery.

Superdawg Drive-In

6363 N. Milwaukee Avenue, Chicago, IL 60646

(773) 736-0660

www.superdawg.com

Superdawg has been in operation since 1948, and it still operates as a real drive-in, including carhop service. Their Chicago-style dogs come with a twist—they include a tomatillo.

Wiener's Circle

2622 N. Clark Street, Chicago, IL 60614

(773) 477-7444

Wiener's Circle is not a place for the timid to dine, especially when the late-night crowd surges through the door. Arguments between customers and staff are expected, and it's all part of the fun—at least for those with spunk.

Chicago-style Hot Dogs

Vienna hot dogs, steamed or charbroiled
Poppy seed hot dog buns, steamed
Plain yellow mustard
Bright green sweet pickle relish
Chopped onion
1 dill pickle spear per dog
2 fresh tomato wedges or slices per dog
2 sport peppers per dog
Celery salt

Place hot dogs in buns and top with mustard, relish, onion, pickle spear, tomato, and sport peppers. Sprinkle lightly with celery salt and serve immediately.

Sources: Vienna Beef brand hot dogs are the frank of choice for most Chicago hot dog restaurants. For retail locations, contact the following:

Vienna Beef
2501 N. Damen Avenue, Chicago, IL 60647
(773) 278-7800
www.viennabeef.com

Poppy seed buns are considered de rigueur for a Chicago-style dog. The Alpha Baking Company manufactures both Mary Ann and Rosen brand buns. For retail locations, contact the following:

Alpha Baking Company, Inc.
4545 W. Lyndl, Chicago, IL 60607
www.alphabaking.com

Sport peppers can be ordered from:

Vincent Formusa Company
710 W. Grand Avenue, Chicago, IL 60610
Telephone: (312) 421-0485
www.marconi-food.com

The bright green relish used on Chicago-style dogs is manufactured by B&G Foods as B&G Emerald Relish. Their website, www.bgfoods.com has a link to www.mybrandsinc.com where it can be ordered if it's not stocked by a local retail market or contact B&G at (888) 281-6400.

Red Hots & Hot Tamales

Chicago hot dog eateries typically include tamales on their menu. According to food historian Barry Popik, this isn't anything new. He references a piece entitled "Red Hot Red Hots: Scare for Everybody for Just a Minute" in the February 16, 1900, edition of the Decatur, Illinois, *Daily Register* that stated, "Tom Busby, the red hot and tamale vendor at Bradley Bros.' Corner, had some of the reddest hot red hots that the Decatur market ever knew last night for a short time. The fire department had to be called to cool them off and then Tom went out of business." Although Chicago has a significant Latino population and plenty of restaurants and vendors selling traditional corn husk–wrapped tamales, the slim version sold in the city's hot dog joints are typically wrapped in parchment. For information on how to purchase these tamales, contact the following company:

Supreme Frozen Products Inc.

5813 W. Grand Avenue, Chicago, IL 60639

(773) 622-3777, www. supremetamale.com

More Cool Dogs in Illinois

Hot Doug's

3324 N. California Street, Chicago, IL 60618

(773) 279-9550

www.hotdougs.com

Checkout Doug's french fries cooked in rendered duck fat!

Jim's Original Hot Dog

700 W. O'Brien Street, Chicago, IL 60607

(312) 733-7820

"Maxwell Street Polish," a polish sausage version of the Chicago dog.

Cozy Drive-In

2935 South 6th Street (Route 66), Springfield, IL 62703

(217) 525-1992

www.cozydogdrivein.com

Home of the Cozy Dog corn dog since 1949.

Indiana

B & K Drive-In

1208 S. Heaton Street, Knox, IN 46534

(574) 772-4888

At one time, there were two hundred thirty-eight B & K Drive-Ins around Indiana, and one can still find a few franchises where old-fashioned carhop service, great hot dogs, and thirst-quenching root beer are enjoyed. Melvin and Mary Bergerson founded B & K, which stands for Bergerson & Kenefick, in the mid-1940s in Michigan City, Indiana. The Bergerson's son Michael remembers that it was his mother who devised the famous B & K Spanish sauce recipe, similar to a mild Coney sauce. At the B & K Drive-In located in Knox, Indiana, "Spanish dogs" remain a popular menu item. They also earn four paws up for holding Dog Days throughout August and donating a percentage of hot dog sales to the Starke County Humane Society.

B & K Spanish Hot Dogs

This is an adaptation of several popular copycat recipes for B & K's famous Coney-style sauce.

Spanish Sauce

1 pound (80 percent lean) ground beef
3/4 cup water
3/4 cup beef broth
1 cup ketchup
2 1/2 teaspoons quality chili powder
1 tablespoon white vinegar
1/4 cup diced onion
1/2 teaspoon salt

In a large, heavy saucepan, mix the ground beef with the water and beef broth, using a slotted spoon so the beef breaks up very fine. Add remaining ingredients and mix well. Cook the sauce over very low heat, uncovered and stirring frequently, for 1 hour and 15 minutes or until mixture is thick. Yield: 3 cups.

Assembly

Hot dogs, steamed
Hot dog buns, steamed
Spanish Sauce
Plain yellow mustard
Chopped onion

Place hot dogs in buns. Top with Spanish Sauce, mustard, and onion and serve immediately.

Michigan

Michigan abounds with eateries serving Coney Island hot dogs; there are hundreds of such restaurants in Detroit alone. Many were established, and are still owned, by Greeks whose forebears arrived in Michigan around 1900. Greek immigrants, having been introduced to hot dogs in New York, developed a unique chili sauce as a condiment and subsequently established hot dog eateries in various cities throughout the country. Coney Island hot dogs are characterized by franks that are usually grilled and served on warm, steamed buns, then topped with Coney Island chili, freshly chopped onion, and plain yellow mustard. The different secret chili recipes vary from restaurant to restaurant. In Detroit, the Coney sauce is more spicy and "wet," meaning that it's not as thick as the "dry," more meaty sauce served in cities like Flint, Michigan. The following is a very brief sampling of Michigan's famous Coney Island hot dog establishments.

American Coney Island
114 W. Lafayette, Detroit, MI 48226
(313) 961-7758
www.americanconeyisland.com

Angelo's Coney Island
1816 Davison Road, Flint, MI 48506
(810) 238-3761
www.angelosconeyisland.com

Duly's Place
5458 W. Vernor Highway, Detroit, MI 48209
(313) 554-3076

Genie's Wienies Coney Island
11608 Conant Street, Detroit, MI 48212
(313) 892-7422

Lafayette Coney Island
118 W. Lafayette Blvd., Detroit, MI 48226
(313) 964-8198

Todoroff's Original Coney Island
211 E. Ganson Street, Jackson, MI 49201
(517) 787-6168
www.todoroffs.com

Flint, Michigan's Coney Island Hot Dogs

Flint's favorite Coney sauce comes highly recommended by resident hot dog fan Donna McDaniel. This is an adaptation of a recipe that has often been featured in the *Flint Journal* over the years.

Flint Coney Sauce

2 tablespoons butter or margarine

1 1/2 pounds (80 percent lean) ground beef

2 medium onions, chopped

1 or 2 cloves garlic, minced, to taste

1 teaspoon ground black pepper

1 teaspoon salt

2 tablespoons quality chili powder

1 tablespoon plain yellow mustard

1 (6-ounce) can tomato paste

3/4 cup water

4 Koegel wieners or use a similar pork-and-beef brand

Combine all ingredients except the wieners in a heavy medium saucepan and mix well to break up the beef. Simmer the mixture over low heat for about 20 minutes or until thick. Grind up the wieners or pulse them 12 to 14 times in a food processor.

If natural casing wieners are used, be sure to remove the casing before grinding them. Add ground wieners to the sauce, mix well, and simmer over low heat for 15 minutes. Yield: about 6 cups.

Assembly

Hot dogs, such a Koegel's pork-and-beef, grilled

Hot dog buns, steamed

Plain yellow mustard

Flint Coney Sauce

Chopped onion

Place hot dogs in buns and top with mustard, Flint Coney Sauce, and onion. Serve immediately.

Note: The use of ground hot dogs in Coney sauce may seem unusual, but it's actually a common practice that enhances the hot dog flavor while making use of left over hot dogs that might otherwise go to waste.

Source: Koegel frankfurters and Viennas, manufactured in Flint, Michigan, can be purchased from the company's online store: www.koegelmeats.com.

Minnesota

Minnesota State Fair

1265 North Snelling Avenue, St. Paul, MN 55108

(651) 288-4400

www.mnstatefair.org

While sophisticates of the Twin Cities enjoy their favorite Chicago-style dogs, others in Minnesota quietly nurse a year-long craving for the pronto pups at the annual Minnesota State Fair in St. Paul. Jack and Gladys Karnis first introduced pronto pups to the Minnesota State Fair in 1947. Granted, there are other culinary delights at the fair, like foot-long hot dogs, corn on the cob, and pork chops, but it's the pronto pup stands, advertising their "Banquet on a Stick," that steal the show. In 2003, fairgoers consumed 515,900 pronto pups. Impaled on sticks, the pups are dunked into a batter of flour and cornmeal and deep-fried.

Pronto Pups

Pronto Pup Batter

3/4 cup plus 2 tablespoons all-purpose flour
1/2 cup cornmeal
3 tablespoons sugar
1 teaspoon salt
1 teaspoon baking powder
1 egg, lightly beaten
1/2 cup plus 3 tablespoons milk

In a large mixing bowl, combine the flour, cornmeal, sugar, salt, and baking powder. In a small mixing bowl, whisk together the egg and milk. Stir the milk mixture into the flour mixture; it should be the consistency of pancake batter.

Assembly

Canola oil for deep-frying
6 to 8 hot dogs, depending on size
Pronto Pup Batter
Plain yellow mustard (optional)

In a deep pot or frying pan, heat the oil to 375 degrees. Dip hot dogs in the batter to evenly cover and fry them, two at a time, until golden, about 2 to 3 minutes. Remove and drain on paper towels. Serve immediately with mustard, if desired. Serves 6 to 8.

Note: If desired, wooden sticks may be inserted into the hot dogs before they are battered and deep-fried.

Missouri

Woofie's Hot Dogs

1919 Woodson Road, Overland, MO 63114

(314) 426-6291

Established in 1977, Woofie's is a legend among hot dog lovers, and it's a St. Louis institution. Just the sight of the bright yellow-and-orange building brings a smile to one's face, and the hot dogs served up at Woofie's are delicious. They serve a mean Chicago-style dog plus Coneys and cheese dogs. But it's the innovative franks at Woofie's that are real attention grabbers. The Reuben dog is topped with Swiss cheese, Thousand Island dressing, pickle, and sauerkraut. The Danny Dog is a corn dog served up with chili and onions. And then there's the Kathy Dog, a perennial favorite.

A Great Woofie's-style Kathy Dog

Vienna beef hot dogs, steamed

Hot dog buns, steamed

Melted cheddar cheese

Plain yellow mustard

1 kosher dill pickle spear per dog

1 strip bacon per dog, fried crisp and drained

Place hot dogs in steamed buns and top each with melted cheddar cheese, mustard, pickle, and bacon. Serve immediately.

Ohio

Cincinnati, Ohio, claims to be the chili capital of the United States. That claim is based on ergonomics (the city has more chili parlors per square mile and per capita than any other in the United States) and pure hometown pride. But when a Cincinnatian talks about chili, it's far from the typical version associated with Texas or the American Southwest. This is chili with a definite Greek twist.

According to food writer Cliffe Lowe, "Tom" Athanas Kiradjieff, a Macedonian immigrant, created Cincinnati chili. Kiradjieff, like many other immigrants, entered America via New York where he became familiar with the hot dog and likely heard stories of other immigrants who had established successful businesses based on the popular sandwich. In 1922, Kiradjieff set up a hot dog stand in Cincinnati, selling franks and Greek food, and named it Empress; according to John Mariani in *The Encyclopedia of American Food & Drink*, the stand was named after the Empress Burlesque Theater that was located in the same building. Kiradjieff revised a traditional Greek stew recipe, flavored with cinnamon and cloves, substituting ground beef and adding chili powder. The result was a unique mixture that doesn't taste like typical American chili. Kiradjieff sold the stew-like mixture served over hot dogs (called Coney's) as well as spaghetti. Empress chili became popular, and Kiradjieff's Cincinnati-style chili was also served as it is today: two-way (spaghetti topped with chili); three-way (spaghetti topped with chili and grated cheddar cheese); four-way (spaghetti topped with chili, grated cheddar cheese, and diced onion); and five-way (spaghetti topped with chili, grated cheddar cheese, diced onion, and kidney beans). Among a host of chili parlors in the Cincinnati area, the following restaurants are traditional favorites.

Empress Chili (Since 1922)

8340 Vine Street, Cincinnati, OH 45216

(513) 761-5599

Gold Star Chili (Since 1965)

979 Hawthorne Avenue, Cincinnati, OH 45205

(513) 471-2458

www.goldstarchili.com

Skyline Chili (Since 1949)

3714 Warsaw Avenue, Cincinnati, OH 45205

(513) 471-2445

www.skylinechili.com

Cincinnati Coney Dogs

Cliff Lowe's authentic Cincinnati chili recipe, given to him by a Greek gentleman who owned a chili parlor on Cincinnati's Vine Street, is reprinted with permission from Diana Serbe's website www.inmamaskitchen.com.

Cincinnati Chili

2 pounds (80 percent lean) ground beef

3 cups cold water

2 large onions, finely chopped

2 teaspoons garlic powder or granules

1 ounce unsweetened baking chocolate,
    coarsely chopped

1/4 cup quality chili powder

1 1/2 teaspoons ground allspice

1/2 teaspoon ground cinnamon

1 teaspoon ground cumin

1/4 teaspoon ground cloves

1 1/2 teaspoons salt

2 bay leaves

1 (6-ounce) can tomato paste

1 tablespoon red wine vinegar

In a large, 6-quart Dutch oven or pot, combine ground beef with water, and stir it well with a slotted spoon to break up the meat. The mixture will be quite thick; do not add any additional water. Add remaining ingredients and stir well. Place pot over high heat and bring to a boil; lower heat, cover, and cook for 1 hour and 40 minutes, stirring every 15 minutes. Remove cover, remove bay leaves, and cook for 20 minutes longer or until the mixture is very thick. Yield: about 7 cups.

Assembly

Hot dogs, steamed or grilled

Hot dog buns, steamed

Cincinnati Chili

Plain yellow mustard

Chopped onions

Grated cheddar cheese

Place hot dogs in buns and top with Cincinnati Chili, mustard, onions, and cheese. Serve immediately.

Tony Packo's Café

1902 Front Street, Toledo, OH 43605

(419) 885-4500

www.tonypackos.com

M*A*S*H fans will immediately recognize Tony Packo's—
the zany character Corporal Max Klinger was from Toledo
and he advised a newsman, "If you're ever in Toledo,
Ohio, on the Hungarian side of town, Tony Packo's got
the greatest Hungarian hot dogs. Thirty-five cents . . ."
Although the price has gone up since those days, the dogs
are still great at Tony Packo's, which is also known for the
many celebrity-autographed hot dog buns that decorate the
walls of the restaurant. The son of a Hungarian immigrant,
Tony Packo was a former factory worker who opened his
restaurant in 1932, during the worst part of the depression.
Times were hard and money was tight so Tony split his
homemade sausages in half, placed them in buns, and
topped them with a spicy meat sauce to give them a bit

more heft. He called them "Hungarian hot dogs" and the neighborhood loved the new sandwich. Today, Tony
Packo's still serves what has been called Toledo's signature hot dog. The secret-recipe sauce can be ordered
from the Tony Packo's website.

Packo's-style Hungarian Hot Dogs

Toledo, Ohio, ex-patriots claim this sauce delivers a taste of Tony Packo's when they can't enjoy the real thing. This is an adaptation of several traditional copycat recipes.

Hungarian-style Sauce

1 pound (80 percent lean) ground beef
1 1/2 cups beef broth, or more to taste
3/4 teaspoon dried thyme leaves
3/4 teaspoon ground cumin
1 tablespoon plus 1 1/2 teaspoons chili powder
1 1/2 teaspoons ground black pepper
1 1/2 teaspoons paprika
1/2 teaspoon onion powder
1/8 teaspoon ground cayenne pepper
1/2 teaspoon brown sugar
2 cloves garlic, minced

In a medium saucepan, combine beef and broth and mix well with a slotted spoon to break up the beef. Add remaining ingredients and mix well. Simmer the mixture, uncovered, over medium-low heat, stirring frequently, for 1 1/2 hours, or until thick; this is a medium-dry sauce, so add more beef broth if preferred. Yield: about 1 cup.

Assembly

Hot dogs, grilled
Hot dog buns, steamed
Hungarian-style Sauce
Plain yellow mustard
Chopped onion

Place hot dogs in buns and top with Hungarian-style Sauce, mustard, and onion. Serve immediately.

Wisconsin

The Charcoal Inn

1637 Geele Avenue, Sheboygan, WI 53083

(920) 458-1147

and

1313 S. Eighth Street, Sheboygan, WI 53081

(920) 458-6988

Wisconsin has its share of corn dogs, Chicago-style hot dogs, and Coneys, but anyone wanting to eat in the true native style will happily take a bit of a detour when it comes to hot dogs. That's because Wisconsin is the home of "the best of the wurst"—as in bratwurst. And the bratwurst of choice is manufactured by Usinger's, a German sausage maker that also happens to make what some people swear are the best all-beef franks and wieners available.

Grilled Brats, Sheboygan-style

4 fresh bratwurst sausages
1 (12-ounce) bottle of beer (do not use light beer)
Softened butter
4 bratwurst rolls, crusty rolls, or hot dog rolls
German- or Dijon-style mustard (or mustard of choice)
Chopped fresh onion
Pickles
Sauerkraut (optional), plain or heated (see page 38)

Pierce each bratwurst four times with a fork and place in a frying pan large enough to hold them in one layer. Add beer, bring to a boil over medium heat, and let simmer for 15 to 20 minutes. Heat grill. Drain bratwurst and place on grill over medium-high heat. Grill for about 10 minutes or until well browned.

Meanwhile, lightly butter the rolls. Just before brats are done, place rolls under a preheated broiler, or facedown on the grill, until they are golden brown. Place brats in rolls and serve with mustard, onion, and pickles or Sauerkraut, if desired. Note that Sheboyganites are likely to douse their bratwurst sandwiches with plenty of hot melted butter. Serves 4.

Source: Delicious bratwurst and other sausages can be ordered from:

Usinger's Famous Sausage
1030 N. Old World Third Street
Milwaukee, WI 53203
(800) 558-9998 or (414) 276-9105
www.usinger.com

CHAPTER 5

Hot Dogs of The Great Plains: Corn Dogs, Chile Dogs, and Buffalo Dogs

A historical great of South Dakota and the Great Plains: Mount Rushmore.

The Great Plains of the United States is distinguished by its enormous corn production, and the foodways of the region clearly reflect the fact that corn is a primary cooking staple. Here, rolls or buns are eschewed in favor of cornmeal mixtures in which hot dogs are encased and then deep-fried, resulting in corn dogs and pronto pups that are sold by food concessions throughout the grounds of every state fair in the region. In the Dakotas, buffalo dogs frequently upstage beef-and-pork hot dogs, the delicious result of an increased number of buffalo ranches as well as product creativity. Down in Oklahoma, Coney Island-style hot dogs, introduced by Greek immigrants decades ago, remain very popular, and lip-smacking Southwestern chili dogs, packing plenty of heat, show that area's close ties to food with a south-of-the-border influence.

Iowa

Iowa State Fair

P.O. Box 51730, Des Moines, IA 50317-0003

(515) 262-3111

www.iowastatefair.org

It's all about corn dogs in Iowa; somehow, pronto pups (lacking the descriptive word corn) never quite made the grade. Perhaps that's because Iowa is the leading producer of corn in the United States, a tradition that dates back to the Ioway Indians who cultivated corn long before the arrival of the white man. Folks in "The Corn State" are liable to be very loyal to their number-one product, as evidenced by favorite foods like kettle corn, corn bread, creamed corn, corn on the cob, and yes, corn dogs. The latter are sold at diners and fast food stands, such as the Maid-Rite chain, throughout the state, and Iowa housewives, who tend to excel in the kitchen, are likely to whip up a batch of them for supper even in the dead of winter when Iowa celebrates corn month.

Kansas

Kansas State Fair

2000 N. Poplar Street, Hutchinson, KS 67502

(620) 669-3600

www.kansasstatefair.com

The annual Kansas State Fair, held in September, celebrates the agricultural heritage of "The Wheat State." The leading producer of wheat in America, Kansas is also a significant producer of corn, and residents love their corn dogs. However, one is advised to refer to the deep-fried Kansas version as a pronto pup. Fair-goers seeking their annual pronto pup fix look for the bright yellow stands, and many just follow the aroma that permeates the fairgrounds. The freshly cooked, golden-hued beauties, known as "a banquet on a stick," are served up hot and sizzling to folks who promptly down them un-garnished or perhaps, with a quick smear of mustard.

Nebraska

Nebraska State Fair

P. O. Box 81223, Lincoln, NE 68501

(402) 474-5371

www.statefair.org

Nebraskans look forward to late August when the state fair opens its gates. Established in 1868, the fair provides a showcase for the achievements of Nebraskans as well as a family education and entertainment venue. Known as "The Cornhusker State," a term that dates to the harvesting or husking of corn by hand before a mechanical means was devised, Nebraska's number-one crop covers more than eight million acres in the Great Plains area of the state. Like their counterparts in Iowa, Nebraskans love their corn dogs, which taste especially good at the Nebraska State Fair.

North Dakota

North Dakota State Fair

2005 Burdick Expressway East, P.O. Box 1796. Minot, ND 58702

(701) 857-7620

www.ndstatefair.org

North Dakota borders on the American corn and pork belt, and the southeastern portion of the state is an area that specializes in corn production, so it's no wonder that folks here enjoy a corn dog or two. The Pride of Dakota Day at the fair features state products, including Cloverdale Foods Company, a North Dakota meat processor that makes an all-beef frank sold in markets in the upper Midwest. Hot dog "feeds" are popular entertainment and fund-raising venues in North Dakota, but when the state fair is in full swing in July, attendees can be seen munching contentedly on their corn dogs.

State Fair Corn Dogs

Canola oil for deep-frying
1/2 cup all-purpose flour
1/2 cup yellow cornmeal
1 tablespoon sugar
1 teaspoon baking powder
1/2 teaspoon salt
1 teaspoon dry mustard
1/2 cup milk
1 egg
1 tablespoon vegetable shortening
    (such as Crisco), melted
6 hot dogs
Plain yellow or spicy brown mustard

In a deep pot, heat oil to 375 degrees. In a bowl, mix together the flour, cornmeal, sugar, baking powder, salt, and dry mustard. In a separate bowl, whisk together the milk, egg, and shortening and add it to the flour mixture, stirring until smooth. Place the mixture in a deep pie pan. Dry hot dogs with paper towels. Dip hot dogs into batter to evenly coat and carefully place into hot oil, cooking two at a time. Deep-fry 2 to 3 minutes, or until golden brown, turning them carefully with tongs to brown all sides. Remove from oil and drain on paper towels. Serve immediately with the mustard. Serves 6.

Note: If desired, wooden sticks may be inserted into the hot dogs before they are battered and deep-fried.

Oklahoma

Coney I-Lander

7408 E. Admiral Place, Tulsa, OK 74115

(918) 836-2336

Multiple locations

The entry for *chili* in the Oklahoma Historical Society's *Encyclopedia of Oklahoma History and Culture* observes that Greek-style chili, similar to that served in Cincinnati, Ohio, was introduced in Oklahoma in the mid-1920s. Christ Economou, a Greek immigrant, founded the Coney Island in Tulsa in 1926 where chili, containing cinnamon, chili powder, paprika, and red pepper, was served over hot dogs. Economou had operated hot dog eateries in Dallas and Houston, and he apparently added traditional Greek spices to beanless Texas chili. In 1982, the Tulsa restaurant was re-named Coney I-Lander and it has become a multi-location franchise, still greatly favored by Tulsan's. It's one of many similar Coney Island hot dog establishments, most run by Greeks, in Oklahoma.

Eskimo Joe's

501 W. Elm, Stillwater, OK 74074

(405) 372-8896

wwww.eskimojoes.com

In Stillwater, Oklahoma, it's all about Eskimo Joe's, a juke joint that pulls in the crowds simply because it offers great service and a happy fun-filled atmosphere along with terrific food. Stan Clark and Steve File founded Eskimo Joe's as a bar in 1975, catering to students at nearby Oklahoma State University. T-shirts with the logo of a grinning Eskimo and his dog Buffy helped establish immediate name recognition. Clark bought out his partner in 1978, and in 1984, after Oklahoma raised the drinking age to twenty-one, he started selling food in order to survive.

The early menu at Eskimo Joe's featured two items that became signature dishes on the menu: Joe's Dog, smothered in a spicy, Oklahoma-style chili that includes beans; and fresh-cut cheese fries topped with melted Monterey Jack and cheddar cheeses and bacon bits, served with a side of ranch dressing for dipping, which Eskimo Joe's proclaims are endorsed by former President George H.W. Bush.

Eskimo Joe's World Famous Chili Dogs

Eskimo Joe's fans unable to regularly visit the pub claim that this chili recipe, adapted from a copycat version, approximates the real thing, and they enjoy it by the bowl or as a topping for hot dogs. Note that Eskimo Joe's uses kidney beans rather than the red chili beans called for here.

Chili

1 1/2 pounds (90 percent lean) ground beef
1 tablespoon vegetable oil
1/2 cup chopped green bell pepper
1/2 cup chopped onion
1 (4-ounce) can diced green chiles
1 (10-ounce) can diced tomatoes with green chiles
1 (16-ounce) can Bush's Red Chili Beans in
    Hot Sauce (see note)
1 (8-ounce) can tomato sauce
2 tablespoons quality chili powder
1 teaspoon ground cumin seed
1/2 teaspoon salt
1 teaspoon dried oregano
1 1/2 teaspoons ground black pepper
1/4 teaspoon ground cayenne pepper
1 1/4 cups beef broth

In a deep, heavy frying pan or medium pot, brown the beef over medium-high heat, stirring with a slotted spoon to break it up.

Drain fat and then place beef in a bowl; set aside. Add the oil to the pan and sauté the bell pepper and onion over low heat just until it begins to soften. Return the beef to the pan, and add all remaining ingredients, mixing well. Bring the chili to a boil, lower heat, and simmer, stirring frequently, for 1 hour and 15 minutes or until it thickens. Yield: about 5 cups.

Assembly

Hot dogs, grilled
Hot dog rolls, toasted
Chili

Place hot dogs in buns, top with chili, and serve immediately.

Note: The use of Bush's Red Chili Beans in Hot Sauce delivers a spicy chili; if less spice is preferred, use Bush's Red Chili Beans in Mild Sauce or use plain chili beans without sauce.

South Dakota

Wall Drug Store

510 Main Street, Wall, SD 57790

(605) 279-2175

www.walldrug.com

South Dakota is a cattle state. Like Montana, it has more cattle than people. But with over 155 producers raising approximately 30,000 head of buffalo, the state is also known for its prime buffalo meat, much of which is certified organic. And buffalo meat hot dogs from Western Buffalo Meats in Rapid City, South Dakota, have also become a specialty of the house at the famous Wall Drug Store in Wall, South Dakota.

Ted and Dorothy Husted established Wall Drug in 1931. Unfortunately, tourists destined for the Black Hills and Badlands region of the state whizzed by the small store in the one-horse town of Wall and business languished. Finally, Dorothy suggested that surely all those travelers must be thirsty, and the Husteds erected signs advertising free ice water. The marketing gimmick was a success, and business boomed.

Today, the Wall Drug complex is humongous and attracts over a million people every year. The company is now under the third-generation direction of Teddy Husted, who exhibits all the personality and marketing genius of the late Ted Husted, his grandfather. Wall Drug is a kitschy mix of museum, souvenirs, and more. Free ice water is still available out in the "backyard," and at Wall Drug Café, coffee is only five cents a cup. Diners feast on awesome quarter-pound, deep-fried buffalo dogs served up with traditional condiments like ketchup, mustard, and relish. Wall also serves a terrific buffalo chili dog.

Deep-fried South Dakota Buffalo Dogs

Canola oil for deep-frying
4 (1/4-pound) buffalo meat dogs
4 hot dog buns
Ketchup
Mustard
Relish

Source: Retail locations for the purchase of buffalo meat hot dogs, as served at Wall Drug, can be obtained from the following:

Western Buffalo Company
1015 E. St. Patrick Street, Rapid City, SD 57709
(800) 247-3263 or (605) 342-0322

In a deep, heavy pot, heat the canola oil to 350 degrees. Carefully add the buffalo meat dogs to the hot oil, and deep-fry for 2 1/2 to 3 minutes. Place the buffalo dogs on buns and serve with ketchup, mustard, and relish.

South Dakota Sweet Cucumber Relish

The ladies of South Dakota still make homemade hot dog relish that's not to be missed. Thanks to Lavonne Riedel of Madison, South Dakota, we found Betty Brookshire who has made this delicious recipe for at least 45 years, proving that South Dakotans relish their tasty traditions. Reprinted with permission from Betty L. Brookshire, Madison, South Dakota.

4 to 6 unpeeled cucumbers (about 3 1/2 cups ground)
6 medium carrots, peeled (about 1 1/2 cups ground)
2 medium onions (about 1 cup ground)
2 tablespoons pickling salt
2 1/2 cups sugar
1 1/2 cups white vinegar
1 1/2 teaspoons celery seed
1 1/2 teaspoons mustard seed

Grind the cucumbers, carrots, and onions, place in a large bowl, and mix well. Stir in the pickling salt, and let the mixture stand for 3 hours; drain well. In a large pot, combine the sugar, vinegar, celery seed, and mustard seed and bring the mixture to a boil. Carefully add the drained vegetables and bring just to a boil. Lower heat and simmer the mixture for 20 minutes. Pack the relish in hot sterile jars, and seal according to manufacturer's instructions. Yield: 6 to 7 pints.

CHAPTER 6

Hot Dogs of the West and Southwest: Some Like it Hot

"Reds" and "hots" have a slightly stronger meaning in this part of the country.

In the American West, frankfurters are typically spiced up with ingredients like chiles and beans that are so much a part of the region's cuisine. This delivers awesome flavors that give new meaning to the word "hot" dog! The Sonora-style hot dogs of Tucson are gussied up with salsa, pinto beans, guacamole, jalepeño peppers, and other fresh tastes typically found in a taco, delivering a walloping great wiener. Various renditions of chili are everywhere, and vendors in Western states proudly feature it as a topping for hot dogs. In Colorado, buffalo dogs are accompanied by the titillating flavor of green pork chili. The deep, earthy flavor of New Mexico red chile enhances the franks at Albquerque's Dog House Drive In. But there's more than chiles. In Utah, barely a hot dog is served without a side of fries accompanied by Utah Fry Sauce. And in Idaho, ingenuity led to the delicious development of the tater dog and a mightly successful street vending business.

Arizona

BK Carne Asada and Hotdogs

5118 S. 12th Avenue, Tucson, AZ 85706

(520) 295-0105

Many popular foods in Arizona reflect the cuisine of the neighboring Mexican state of Sonora, so it's not surprising to find that even the all-American hot dog should succumb to a bit of that influence as well. A true Sonoran-style dog is served in a crusty Mexican bolillo, which is similar to a French roll but a bit sweeter. The hot dog is wrapped in bacon and grilled over charcoal or mesquite and then placed in the bolillo and garnished with standard Mexican toppings that produce a heavenly Southwestern rendition of the humble hot dog.

Sonoran-style Hot Dogs

Pork-and-beef hot dogs

1 slice mesquite-smoked bacon per hot dog
   (or substitute regular bacon)

Bolillos or French-style rolls

Grated Monterey Jack cheese

Ketchup

Tomatillo salsa

Mayonnaise

Shredded lettuce

Chopped fresh tomato

Freshly chopped onion

Whole or refried pinto beans (optional)

Guacamole or avocado slices (optional)

Plain yellow mustard (optional)

Sliced jalapeños (optional)

Prepare an outdoor grill using either charcoal or mesquite. Wrap each hot dog with a slice of bacon and grill until they are cooked through and the bacon is crispy. Place the hot dogs in rolls and garnish with cheese, ketchup, salsa, mayonnaise, lettuce, tomato, and onion. Add any desired optional garnishes and serve immediately.

Colorado

Buffalo Restaurant & Bar

1617 Miner Street, Idaho Springs, CO 80452

(303) 567-2729

www.buffalorestaurant.com

Buffalo Restaurant & Bar is located in historic Idaho Springs. Owned by New West Foods, previously known as the Denver Buffalo Company, there are plenty of buffalo specialties on the menu, including a buffalo meat hot dog topped with a choice of red beef chili, green pork chili, or black bean buffalo chili and, if requested, cheese.

Buffalo Dogs with Green Pork Chili

Green Pork Chili

Vegetable oil

3 tablespoons flour

1 pound pork shoulder, trimmed and cut into 1/4-inch dice

1 medium onion, chopped

2 cloves garlic, chopped

1 cup canned diced tomatoes with green chiles, with juice

4 (4-ounce) cans diced green chiles

2 tablespoons tomato paste

1 1/2 cups beef broth

3/4 teaspoon salt

1/2 teaspoon pepper

1/4 teaspoon ground Mexican oregano

In a deep frying pan, heat 1 tablespoon oil over medium-high heat. Place flour in a ziplock bag and shake the pork cubes to coat. Brown one-third of the cubes in the oil, stirring with a slotted spoon; remove and place in a bowl. Add oil to the skillet, as needed, and brown remaining pork, one-third at a time. Add oil to the frying pan if needed and sauté the onion, stirring occasionally, until soft and translucent. Add garlic the last minute of cooking. Add pork to onion mixture and stir in remaining ingredients. Bring mixture to a boil, lower the heat, and simmer, uncovered and stirring occasionally, for 30 minutes, or until pork is very tender and the mixture has thickened. Yield: about 5 cups.

Assembly

Buffalo meat hot dogs, grilled (see Note)

Hot dog buns, toasted

1/4 cup Green Pork Chili per buffalo dog

2 tablespoons grated cheddar or Monterey Jack cheese per buffalo dog (optional)

Chopped onion (optional)

Place grilled dogs on toasted rolls. Top with the Green Pork Chili, cheese, and onion. Serve immediately.

Note: Buffalo meat is lean and should always be cooked or grilled at a lower temperature and for less time than beef. Be sure to follow package directions for preparation.

The Boardwalk at Coney Island

U.S. Highway 285 (just west of Bailey), Bailey, CO 80422

Jack-n-Grill

2542 Federal Boulevard, Denver, CO 80211

(303) 964- 9544

Idaho

Meat N' Taters (street vendor)

Downtown Boise, Southeast Corner of 6th and Main Streets, Boise, ID

No public phone

Idaho's tourism department bills the state as "Great Potatoes—Tasty Destinations" and when it comes to a search for great hot dogs, the slogan provides a terrific tip. Folks in Idaho are partial to corn dogs and pronto pups, but their real loyalty lies with potatoes—after all, the state produces 13.8 billion pounds annually. It was thus not a huge surprise to discover that a favorite treat in Boise is the Tater Dog, created by Eric Savage, proprietor of Meat N' Taters, a food cart located on the southeast corner of 6th and Main Streets in downtown Boise. Eric says that his tater dogs were developed out of necessity one evening when he had dinner guests. Noting that the potatoes were nearly baked, Eric went out to prepare the steaks that had been left by the grill, only to discover his dog had devoured them. With nothing else in the larder, he quickly cut the potatoes into long strips, dipped them in his barbecue sauce, and placed them on the grill. Eric's guests were so impressed they suggested that he consider selling barbecued potatoes. It wasn't long before Eric traded his software company for a street vending cart and the rest, as they say, is history.

Known as "the yellow man" or "the tater man," Eric, dressed in a yellow shirt, serves the evening bar crowds that flock to the downtown district. Hours of operation are from 10:00 p.m. to 4:00 a.m. on

Wednesdays, Fridays, and Saturdays in the summer, and Fridays and Saturdays in the winter. Folks who don't wish to venture downtown send a Yellow Cab to pick up their orders from Eric's bright yellow cart topped with an equally bright yellow umbrella. Yep, it's all about yellow; according to Eric, it's the color that makes us salivate. Eric apparently knows what he's doing—he has sold 40 tons of potatoes in eight years!

Well, back to the Tater Dog. Clearly, it's not a hot dog at all, although it's certainly a terrific vegetarian alternative. Giant Idaho potatoes that have been baked, cut in quarters, and marinated in a proprietary, hickory smoke–flavored barbecue sauce are used in the Tater Dog. The potatoes are grilled on site, and a full quarter potato is popped into a hot dog bun and served up with a choice of traditional condiments, including mustard, ketchup, relish, onion, cheese, and jalapeño peppers. Of course, one isn't limited to Tater Dogs from the Meat 'N' Taters cart. The creative menu also includes hot dogs, chorizo, and other sausages. And there are specialties like Chick-Bacon on Tater (rolled up in a tortilla), Tater Tacos, and Chorizo Tater Tacos, all served up with potato wedges marinated in that fabulous secret barbecue sauce.

Meat 'N' Taters' Tater Dog

1 large russet potato
Thick hickory-flavored barbecue sauce, such as
    KC Masterpiece Hickory Brown Sugar
Olive oil
4 quality hot dog buns

Choice of condiments:
    Plain yellow mustard
    Ketchup
    Fresh chopped onions
    Relish
    Quality squeeze-type nacho cheese or grated cheddar
    Sliced jalapeño peppers

Preheat oven to 425 degrees and bake the potato until it's slightly tender but still a bit firm. Remove the potato from the oven and let cool until it's just warm to the touch. Quarter the potato lengthwise and carefully prick the quarters three or four times with a fork; dip the quarters in the barbecue sauce until well covered on all sides. Place potatoes on a baking sheet and refrigerate them, covered, overnight or at least 3 hours, allowing the sauce to be absorbed. When ready to serve, heat an outdoor grill and lightly brush the grid with olive oil. Grill the potato wedges over medium-low heat at 300 degrees for about 30 minutes or until hot and crusty-browned on all sides. If desired, brown the buns a bit on the grill. Place each potato wedge in a hot dog bun and serve with a choice of condiments. Serves 4.

Montana

Wild Mile Deli

435 Bridge Street, Bigfork, MT 59911

(406) 837-3354

www.wildmiledeli.com

Located in northwestern Montana, the town of Bigfork attracts visitors to Glacier National Park and the Bob Marshall and Swan Wilderness areas. The Swan River Wild Mile Corridor, a natural gorge carved through the backbone of the Mission Mountain Range, flows into Flathead Lake at Bigfork, and for thirty years, the area has hosted the kayak races in the Bigfork Whitewater Festival held every June. For more sedate visitors, Bigfork offers art galleries, plenty of fishing, and numerous restaurants. Anyone seeking casual dining is well advised to head for the Wild Mile Deli, specializing in German cuisine and just the place for great wieners or sausages like bratwurst, bockwurst, and knackwurst, which come from Bavarian Meat Products in Seattle, Washington. Proprietor Michael Beaubien serves them up on French rolls accompanied by terrific winekraut and deli mustard, both of which are made in-house. Winekraut is sauerkraut that has fermented in white wine, and it's a favored variety among kraut aficionados. Beaubein's deli mustard is a mixture of yellow and stone-ground mustards, and it can be purchased to take home.

Winekraut Wieners

Pork-and-beef wieners, steamed

French rolls, heated

1/3 cup heated quality winekraut
(such as the Steinfeld's brand) per wiener

Deli-style (brown) mustard

Place steamed wieners in heated rolls, garnish with winekraut and mustard to taste. Serve immediately.

Nevada

Mr. Hot Dog

730 E. Flamingo Road, Las Vegas, NV 89119

(702) 731-6550

Multiple Locations

Max Jacobson, food writer for the *Las Vegas Weekly*, recently pointed out that there was a proliferation of hot dog eateries in "Sin City." Jacobson speculated that perhaps it was a result of the economy, which may be true, but there's another factor—vacationers and transplants from the East coast can eat fancy food just so long and then they start craving everyday fun food and old favorites like hot dogs. One of the newest hot doggeries in Vegas is Mr. Hot Dog, owned by Tony Davi who originally hails from New York. Manager Mary Rocco, a Chicago native, knew she could run a successful hot dog shop and less than a year after establishing the original store on Flamingo Road, two new Mr. Hot Dog locations have opened. Mary attributes their success to great dogs and friendly service that attracts visitors and repeat business from retirees who like the family atmosphere. After all, says Mary, "Food brings people together."

Mr. Hot Dog features Sabrett hot dogs so beloved by New Yorkers; the dogs are steamed and served in several different ways, including the original Coney Island–style with mustard and kraut, and Chicago-style. The tasty UNLV Rebel Dog comes with bacon and a nicely spiced homemade, beanless chili, while the Mexican Dog delivers up favorite flavors of the Southwest.

Mexican Dogs

Sabrett hot dogs, steamed

Hot dog buns, toasted

2 to 3 tablespoons heated refried beans per dog

2 to 3 tablespoons grated cheddar cheese per dog

Freshly chopped onions

Salsa, to taste

Whole pickled jalapeño peppers

Place steamed dogs on toasted buns. Top with refried beans, cheese, onion, and salsa and garnish with a pickled jalapeño pepper. Serve immediately.

New Mexico

Dog House Drive In

1216 Central Avenue, SW, Albuquerque, NM 87102

(505) 243-1019

When it comes to finding the classic New Mexico hot dog, the hands-down favorite is the Dog House Drive In. The Mead family established this Route 66 institution in downtown Albuquerque around 1940, and Jim and Pat Hartley have owned it for the past 40 years. The humble Dog House, which may be Albuquerque's oldest drive-in, is easily identified by its vintage neon sign graced by a dachshund wagging its tail and munching on a string of hot dogs. Folks in Albuquerque swear this is the place to get the best chile dog in New Mexico. Note the spelling is chile, not chili, which New Mexico frowns upon as some kind of perverted Tex-Mex soup. New Mexico–style chile has a pretty good kick to it, and that can be a bit startling to visitors. The Dog House franks are served up with a blanket of delicious red chile made from dried New Mexico red chiles, and it contains a bit of ground beef. Jim Hartley says the original owners created the secret recipe, which he acquired when he bought the business. Gold Star brand pork-and-beef wieners are butterflied and grilled, and they are cradled in a bun that has been toasted on the grill to prevent the sauce from soaking into it and becoming soggy. The chile-sauced dogs are typically served with grated cheddar cheese, onion, and mustard. Some patrons claim that the Dog House also serves the best Frito pie in town.

Corn Dogs, New Mexico Style

Corn dog fans are rewarded with a twist to the standard corn dog at the New Mexico State Fair held every September in Albuquerque. The state's signature green chile is mixed into the corn dog batter, producing a spicy, lip-smacking treat.

New Mexico Red Chile Dogs

New Mexico Chile

2 tablespoons bacon drippings

2 tablespoons flour

1/4 cup pure ground mild New Mexico chile (see Note)

2 cups quality beef broth

1/2 teaspoon salt

1 clove garlic, finely chopped

Pinch of ground Mexican oregano

Pinch of ground cumin powder

1 pound (80 percent lean) ground beef

1/2 teaspoon pure ground hot New Mexico chile (optional)

In a medium saucepan, heat bacon drippings over low heat. Whisk in the flour and cook, whisking constantly, for 3 minutes. Remove pan from heat and whisk in the chile powder. Return to medium heat and gradually whisk in the beef broth. Add salt, garlic, oregano, and cumin and mix thoroughly. Cook over medium heat, whisking constantly, for 10 minutes; mixture will thicken. Add ground beef to the chile in four batches, crumbling it up as it's added to the pan, and stir with a slotted spoon to break up the meat as finely as possible. Simmer the mixture an additional 10 minutes. Stir in the hot chile if desired and cook 5 minutes longer. Yield: about 3 cups.

Assembly

Beef-and-pork hot dogs, butterflied and grilled

Hot dog buns, toasted

Plain yellow mustard

New Mexico Chile

Grated cheddar cheese

Chopped onion

Place hot dogs in rolls and top with mustard, New Mexico Chile, cheese, and onion. Serve immediately.

Note: This produces a fairly mild chile; if more heat is desired, substitute a portion of the mild chile with pure ground hot New Mexico chile. Do not substitute regular chile powder; it is not at all comparable to New Mexico ground chile.

Source: New Mexico dried chile and other chile products may be ordered from Lytle Farms at:

Hatch Chile Express

P.O. Box 350, Hatch, NM 87937

(505) 267-3226

hatchchilecom.host-manager.com

Texas

James Coney Island

701 Town & Country, Houston, TX 77079

(713) 932-1500

www.jamesconeyisland.com

James and Tom Papadakis, immigrants from Greece who arrived in New York in the early 1900s, founded James Coney Island in Houston in 1923. Today, the Houston chain is owned by a group of private investors and has twenty-three locations, a testimony to the fact that the company has become a veritable institution in the area. The Coney dogs are grilled and topped with ground beef sauce that closely resembles Texas chili rather than Coney sauce.

Texas Chili Dogs

Texas Hot Dog Chili

Vegetable oil

2 1/2 pounds chuck steak diced into 1/4-inch pieces

1 (32-ounce) container beef broth

2 cups crushed tomatoes with puree

2 tablespoons quality chili powder

1 tablespoon paprika

1 teaspoon onion powder

1 teaspoon garlic powder

1 teaspoon kosher salt

1/4 teaspoon cayenne pepper

In a medium pot, heat 1 tablespoon oil over high heat. Add a handful of beef and brown it quickly, stirring constantly; remove beef place in a bowl. Continue browning beef by the handful, adding 1/2 tablespoon oil per batch when necessary, until all beef has been browned. Return beef to the pot and add beef broth.

Heat just to the boiling point, lower heat to medium-low, and simmer, uncovered, for 30 minutes. Add remaining ingredients, mixing well. Continue cooking over medium-low heat, uncovered and stirring frequently, for 1 1/2 hours, or until mixture is very thick. Yield: 4 cups.

Assembly

Hot dogs, grilled

Hot dog buns, toasted

Texas Hot Dog Chili

Grated cheddar cheese

Chopped onion

Place hot dogs in buns and top with Texas Hot Dog Chili, cheese, and onion. Serve immediately.

Amarillo Cheese Fries and Dip

Robbie Haferkamp puts her culinary expertise to work by creating copycat recipes for dishes from numerous dining establishments, such as the following recipes for taco seasoning (similar to Taco Bell's) and Amarillo Cheese Fries and Dip (similar to The Lone Star Steakhouse & Saloon). Reprinted with permission from *A Way to the Heart: Recipes for the Food Everyone Loves* by Robbie Haferkamp.

Taco Seasoning

2 tablespoons all-purpose flour
2 teaspoons chili powder
1 1/2 teaspoons dried minced onion
1 1/4 teaspoons salt
1 teaspoon paprika
3/4 teaspoon crushed beef bouillon cube
1/4 teaspoon sugar
1/4 teaspoon cayenne pepper
1/4 teaspoon garlic powder
Dash of onion powder

Mix all ingredients together in a small bowl. Store in an airtight container at room temperature. Yield: 1/3 cup.

Dip

1 cup ranch dressing
2 tablespoons plus 1 1/2 teaspoons Taco Seasoning

In a medium bowl, combine ranch dressing and Taco Seasoning. Cover and refrigerate until ready to serve.

Fries

1 (32-ounce) bag frozen spicy fries, such as Ore-Ida Zesties
1/4 cup grated cheddar cheese or more, to taste
1/4 cup grated Monterey Jack cheese or more, to taste
4 strips bacon, cooked crispy, drained, and crumbled

Prepare fries according to package directions and place on a baking sheet. Preheat broiler. Sprinkle cheese and bacon over fries and broil until cheese is melted. Serve immediately with the dip. Serves 6 to 8.

Texas Lays Claim to Corny Dogs

According to legend, Carl and Neil Fletcher invented the corn dog in 1938. The brothers had been offered a booth at Dallas' Texas State Fair, and they needed an interesting product to sell. Recalling a Dallas street vendor who coated wieners in corn batter and then baked them in corn-shaped molds, the Fletchers vowed to simplify the process. They placed the hot dogs on sticks, dipped them in a corn batter, and deep-fried them, easing not only preparation but providing more convenience in eating. The corn dog was initially called "Fletcher's Original State Fair Corny Dog."

Utah

Ab's Drive-In

4591 South 5600 West, West Valley, UT 84120

(801) 968-2130

and

4100 West 4715 South, Salt Lake City, UT 84118

(801) 969-0525

Utah residents love their hot dogs and burgers, and in the face of increasing encroachment by national chains, the locals are anxious to support home grown mom-and-pop style eateries. Ab and Dot Beutler established Ab's Drive-In in 1951 when they hauled an old shack in front of their home and sold burgers, fries, and milk shakes. In 1991, son Bart and his wife Elizabeth took over the business. Since then, Ab's has moved to a spanking-new building and a second location has been opened. The home of the "original West Valley City burger," Ab's is also a favorite place to enjoy a great hot dog. Both corn dogs and foot-long hot dogs are served up with homemade fries and thick, old-fashioned milk shakes.

Utah's Famous Fry Sauce

Don Carlos Edwards opened the first Arctic Circle restaurant in Salt Lake City, Utah, in 1950. Shortly after opening Arctic Circle, Edwards introduced what was initially called "pink sauce." It soon became known as Utah's famous "fry sauce" even though it was virtually unknown outside the state until visitors to the 2002 Olympics began spreading the word. Similar to a smooth Thousand Island dressing, it has been described as a combination of mayonnaise and ketchup. Folks in Utah are addicted to it as a condiment served with french fries for dipping. Home cooks and major chain restaurants alike have imitated Arctic Circle's formula, so the visitor is likely to encounter numerous versions of fry sauce throughout Utah. Mike Thompson, creator and owner of Some Dude's Fry Sauce, spent a year perfecting his recipe that includes tomatoes, Santa Fe chiles, garlic, and secret spices in addition to ketchup and mayonnaise. Both Thompson and Arctic Circle will ship their fry sauce.

Arctic Circle Restaurants

P.O. Box 339, Midvale, UT 84070

www.arcticcirclerest.com

Some Dude's, L.L.C.

1570 South 300 West, Salt Lake City, UT 84115

(888) 33-DUDES

www.somedudesfrysauce.com

Utah Fry Sauce

Mike Thompson of Some Dude's Fry Sauce says it's great served on hot dogs as well as its traditional use for dipping french fries. The following formula is an adaptation of several traditional recipes for fry sauce.

2/3 cup quality mayonnaise, such as Hellman's

1/3 cup ketchup

1/2 teaspoon plain yellow mustard

1/4 teaspoon garlic powder

1/4 teaspoon onion powder

1 teaspoon sweet pickle juice

1/4 teaspoon Frank's Louisiana Hot Sauce

In a medium bowl, whisk all ingredients until smooth. Cover and refrigerate until ready to use. Yield: 3/4 cup.

Wyoming

Piney Creek General Store / Waldorf A'Story

19 N. Piney Road, Story, WY 82842

(307) 683-2400

pineycreekgeneralstore.com

Hot dogs in Wyoming tend to be basic, no-frills fare, served with standard condiments like mustard and relish. Corn dogs are truly haute dog cuisine. Once in a while, there's a great chili dog to be savored, and if it's served in a fun, friendly place, it can be nirvana.

The Piney Creek General Store in Story, Wyoming, is chock-a-block filled with an enormous range of miscellaneous paraphernalia that includes groceries, gourmet cooking ingredients, beer and wine, cast-iron cookware, and kitschy souvenirs and gifts. The store also has a tiny restaurant called the Waldorf A'Story, and savvy travelers on Interstate 90, between the cities of Sheridan and Buffalo, Wyoming, know that it's smart business to schedule a stop here for a bite to eat. As the menu reminds diners, it's only eight to ten minutes from the highway, "Longer from New York . . . but take yer time . . . yer in God's country!"

In 1993, Dick Hoover decided that he needed to escape the heat of Dallas summers, so he bought a dilapidated old building in Story, fixing it up into what his wife, Patty, says looks a bit like the Alamo. Two years after opening the store, Patty rolled out her moose-themed restaurant, cleverly named the Waldorf A'Story. Both the store and the restaurant are open every day of the year except Christmas. During the summer, patrons can dine outdoors amidst splendid views of the Big Horn Mountains. Among a host of delicious sandwiches and sophisticated specials, the intrepid hot dog lover will find the A'Story's delicious chili dog. Patty's Buck Bandana Chili won first place every year from 1997 to 1999 in the chili cook-off at the Sheridan Wyoming Rodeo, and it's not unusual to see diners order both a chili dog and a big bowl of that fabulous chili that includes meat and chili beans.

Buck Bandana Chili Dogs

Reprinted with permission from Patty Hoover, proprietor, Waldorf A'Story, Story, Wyoming.

Buck Bandana Chili

1/3 cup olive oil

1 cup chopped onion

1 tablespoon chopped garlic

4 or 5 jalapeño peppers, seeded, deveined, and finely chopped, to taste

5 pounds ground beef

3 tablespoons cumin powder or more, to taste

1/2 cup plus 2 tablespoons quality chili powder

1 tablespoon plus 2 teaspoons salt

1 tablespoon ground black pepper

2 1/2 teaspoons sugar, or more to taste

1 1/2 teaspoons cayenne pepper, or more to taste

1 tablespoon plus 2 teaspoons Italian seasoning

1 (6-ounce) can tomato paste

1 (6-pound, 12-ounce) can Kuner's Chili Beans in Chili Sauce

1 (6-pound, 6-ounce) can diced tomatoes including juice

1 (64-ounce) can V8 juice

In a large pot, heat the oil over medium heat. Add onion, garlic, and jalapeños and sauté for 5 minutes. Break the ground beef up into small pieces and add to the pot, stirring to combine. Lightly brown the meat, then add the spices. Continue cooking until meat is completely browned. Add tomato paste, chili beans, tomatoes, and V8 juice, stirring to combine all ingredients. Over high heat, bring the mixture to a boil; lower heat and simmer for 1 hour. Taste for seasoning and add more jalapeño or cayenne pepper if desired or add a little more sugar if required. Yield: about 6 quarts.

Assembly

Hot dogs, grilled

Hot dog buns, toasted

Buck Bandana Chili

Place hot dogs in buns, top with Buck Bandana Chili, and serve immediately.

Source: Kuner's chili beans may be ordered from the following:

Faribault Foods
128 NW 15th Street, Faribault, MN 55021
(507) 334-5521
www.faribaultfood.com

Wyoming Beer-Battered Fries

The traditional french fry rises to new heights in Wyoming where people are especially partial to beer-battered fries.

4 cups beer-battered or regular french fries, cooked

1 cup grated jalapeño Monterey Jack cheese

1 cup grated cheddar cheese

4 slices bacon, cooked until crispy, drained, and crumbled

1 heaping tablespoon snipped fresh chives

Place fries on a rimmed baking sheet; sprinkle with cheeses, and place under broiler until cheeses are melted. Remove from boiler, sprinkle with bacon and chives, and serve immediately. Serves 4.

CHAPTER 7

Hot Dogs of the Pacific: Hollywood Glamour Dogs and Succulent Sausage

Pups with a penchant for palm trees and pineapples.

Hot dogs named after celebrities draw a great deal of attention, if not amusement, on the West Coast. A visit to Pink's in Los Angeles is likely to result in spotting a celebrity or two, in addition to enjoying the taste of a hot dog named after a famous person. A concern for healthy eating throughout the American Pacific region attracts many consumers to poultry or vegetarian alternatives to hot dogs. And a burgeoning specialty sausage industry over the past few decades has resulted in a strong market for all sorts of authentic, old world-style sausages as well as savory new creations. In Alaska, one finds all kinds of sausages and hot dogs, including "reindeer sausage" made from domesticated caribou.

Alaska

M.A.'s Gourmet Dogs (seasonal street vendor)

Located in front of the Old Federal Building at

605 W. 4th Street, Anchorage, AK 99501

No public phone

www.masdogs.com

Michael Anderson personifies the hardy, competitive, and entrepreneurial spirit of Alaska. An Oregon native, Michael traveled the world when his father was in the United States Air Force. Twenty-five years ago, he arrived in "The Last Frontier" to work in a salmon cannery, fell in love with the state, and never left. Many people will recall seeing Michael grilling and serving reindeer dogs in PBS' *A Hot Dog Show*. He's still at it. From April 1 to the end of September, Michael's loyal customers are lined up thirty and forty deep during the lunch hour, but the wait isn't long—this is a one-man show and fast food cart all rolled into one. Regular customers are rewarded for their loyalty—with the "frequent wiener card," every eleventh dog is free. And then there's the daily "Lucky Dog," when a repeat customer is pulled to the front of the line and rewarded with a free lunch just for being patient. Of course, there's a sign that says, "Hugs can influence the judge." Locals love it and tourists get a good laugh.

M.A.'s Gourmet Dogs is all about variety and quality (flavored with a few chuckles), and the menu makes choosing difficult with offerings that include Sinai 48 kosher polish-and-beef dogs, German bratwurst, Louisiana hot links, Italian sausage, chicken linguica, and reindeer sausage (which is actually made from Alaskan domesticated caribou). The dogs and sausages are sliced open and kept warm in the cart's boiler filled with specially flavored water that Michael jokingly refers to as "crack water." They're finished off on the grill and served in a sturdy, steamed bun that resembles a baguette, ensuring the roll holds up once condiments are applied. And the array of condiments is as impressive as the dog menu, including standards like ketchup, sweet green relish, and grated cheddar cheese, plus four kinds of mustard (plain yellow, honey, brown, and Michael's own special creation known as MFG mustard), and Cock brand Thai sriracha chili sauce that has become extremely popular among M.A.'s customers for both its entertainment value and flavor.

Finally, one cannot eat an M.A.'s dog or sausage without Michael Anderson's famous onions cooked on the grill with a judicious splash of Coca-Cola. They are so delicious even kids who vow a hatred of onions chow down on them. Best of all, they're free. But beware—customers who pass on those onions get the famous "M.A. look" of disapproval.

M.A.'s Gourmet Dogs can also be found at the Alaska State Fair (late August to early September), the Iditarod (March), and the Fur Rendezvous in Anchorage (February).

M.A.'s Dogs with M.A.'s Famous Onions

Reprinted with permission from Michael Anderson, proprietor of M.A.'s Gourmet Dogs, Anchorage, AK.

M.A.'s Onions

Vegetable oil
4 medium onions, chopped
Approximately 1 cup Coca-Cola

Grease a grill or frying pan very lightly with vegetable oil. Add onions and grill them over medium-low heat for 2 or 3 minutes. Add 1/4 cup Coca-Cola and continue grilling for 30 minutes or until onions are richly browned, adding 1/4 cup Coca-Cola as needed to keep them moist. Serves 4.

Assembly

Hot dogs or sausage, lightly boiled, split nearly in half, and grilled
Sturdy rolls or mini baguettes, steamed
Thai sriracha chili sauce
Mustard of choice
M.A.'s Onions

Place hot dog or sausage in buns and top with chili sauce, mustard, and M.A.'s Onions. Serve immediately.

Source: Alaskan reindeer sausage can be ordered from:

Alaska Sausage and Seafood Co., Inc.
2914 Arctic Boulevard, Anchorage, AK 99503
(800) 798-3636 or (907) 562-3636
www.alaskasausage.com

California

Pink's Hot Dogs

709 N. La Brea Boulevard, Los Angeles, CA 90038

(323) 931-4223

www.pinkshollywood.com

Pink's is undoubtedly the most famous hot dog stand in California. Paul Pink established the business in 1939 when he sold hot dogs from a pushcart. In 1946, Pink put up a small building, still occupied today, near the corner of La Brea and Melrose, and moved his operation indoors. Long known for its chili dogs based on seven-inch-long Hoffy natural casing all-beef wieners and a decidedly orange-colored chili in steamed buns, the Pink's menu has been expanded in recent years, and it often features franks named after celebrities. Flavors of the Southwest are reflected in offerings like the Bacon Burrito Dog (two dogs, two slices cheese, three slices of bacon, onions, and chili wrapped in a tortilla) and the Guadalajara Dog (topped with onions, relish, tomatoes, and sour cream).

Vegetarians can feast on the Baja Veggie Dog topped with chopped tomatoes, onions, and guacamole, while healthy eaters choose a Turkey Dog. The Pastrami Burrito is likely based on those served at the once popular Oki Dog, and it's a favorite among adventuresome hot dog lovers seeking new taste sensations. Pink's patrons are from all walks of life, but this is Hollywood, so it's not unusual to spot the rich and famous.

Pastrami Burrito Dogs

If a trip to Pink's isn't in the cards, this creation will provide a taste of the famous hot dog stand. A giant tortilla will accommodate a double dog version as served at Pink's, but this single dog version is plenty filling!

1 (12-inch) flour tortilla, heated
1 slice Swiss cheese
1 Hoffy brand natural casing all-beef hot dog, steamed or lightly grilled
2 slices pastrami, cut in strips 1 inch wide and 2 inches long, lightly fried in 1/2 tablespoon butter
1/2 cup beef chili (no beans), heated
Chopped onion to taste

Lay the tortilla out flat. Wrap the cheese slice around the hot dog and place in the center of the tortilla. Top with the pastrami, chili, and onion. Fold in the ends of the tortilla, then fold in the sides as for a burrito. Serve immediately. Serves 1.

Source: Hoffy hot dogs, manufactured by Hoffman Brothers Meat Packing Company, can be ordered from the following:

El Rancho Meat and Provisions Inc.
624 South Santa Anita Avenue, P.O. Box 66087, Arcadia, CA 91066
(800) 325-6805 or (626) 445-1977
www.elranchomeat.com

Tail O' the Pup

Tail O' the Pup was a hot dog stand that looked like a wiener resting in a giant bun topped with mustard. During the 1930s, '40s, and '50s, Los Angeles was awash in what's called programmatic architecture, with buildings designed to reflect the product sold inside. It resulted from the rise of the car culture and the need to quickly capture the attention of people driving by. Los Angeles, one of the first cities to be designed around the automobile as a primary method of transportation, boasted restaurants built in the form of a teepee, a bulldog, and the famous Brown Derby, shaped like a hat. Most of these eateries have vanished. The Tail O' the Pup, designed by architect Milton J. Black and built in 1945, was recently closed. It was a beloved local landmark that had been featured in numerous movies including *Body Double* and *L.A. Story*. It's said that actor Orson Welles ate many a hot dog there, as well as at Pink's. The Pup's signature dogs included the Mexican Ole topped with chili, cheese, and onions, and the Boston Celtic, topped with baked beans, onions, and mustard. Tail O' the Pup was at 329 N. San Vincente, Los Angeles, CA 90048.

Top Dog

2534 Durant Avenue, Berkeley, CA 94704

(501) 843-5967

www.topdoghotdogs.com

Since 1966, a visit to Top Dog has been the equivalent of nirvana for sausage fans. The eatery, now with multiple locations, serves premium products from some of the finest sausage manufacturers to be found. Proprietor Dick Riemann lists an astonishing number of choices on his menu that includes almost every type of wurst one could desire. In addition to quality all-beef franks, one can enjoy Portuguese linguica, Italian Calabrese sausage, and Louisiana hot links. And there's more: mouthwatering turkey sausage made with cilantro and red and green peppers; chicken sausage with lemon and garlic; and smoked chicken sausage with apple. The grilled selections are served on fresh quality buns, and patrons choose from a variety of mustards and condiments that includes a very tasty kraut.

California's Ballpark Garlic Fries

No trip to a California ballpark is complete without a hot dog and an order of garlic fries.

1/4 cup butter
3 cloves garlic, finely chopped
3 tablespoons chopped fresh Italian parsley
4 generous cups thin french fries, cooked until crispy

In a small saucepan over low heat, melt the butter; add the garlic and sauté for 1 minute; add parsley and mix well. Set aside and keep warm. When the fries are cooked, place them in a large bowl, toss with the garlic sauce and serve immediately. Serves 4.

Sources: For those who prefer to grill their franks and sausages at home, Top Dog sells its products uncooked in packages of six or more and they'll also ship sausages; a price list is available on the website along with ordering instructions.

Hawaii

Puka Dog

Poipu Shopping Village, 2360 Kiahuna Plantation Drive, Koloa, Kaua'i, Hawaii 96756

(808) 742-6044

www.pukadog.com

Puka Dog, located on the Garden Island of Kaua'i, is
the creation of owners Dominique and Rick Quinette.
The couple has successfully married the tropical flavors
of the islands with the pedestrian sausage, creating
a taste sensation that's all the rage with residents
and visitors alike. The name "puka" can be a bit
disconcerting at first, so it's important to know that
it's a Hawaiian word that refers to a hole, in this case
the cavity created by a hot spike that's inserted into a
substantial bun, resembling an unsliced hoagie roll.
The toasted cavity is filled with a selection of tropical
sauces and relishes followed by the addition of a grilled
smoked Polish sausage or a veggie dog. It's served up
with freshly squeezed lemonade, and the result is a
unique Hawaiian version of the all-American hot dog.

Puka-style Polish Dogs

The following formulas are not the top-secret recipes used at Puka Dog, but they'll deliver the fresh taste of the islands.

Lemon Garlic Sauce

1/4 cup freshly squeezed lemon juice
4 cloves garlic, chopped
1 teaspoon dried oregano
1 cup extra virgin olive oil

In a food processor, combine lemon juice, garlic, and oregano. Pulse several times to break up the garlic, then process for 1 minute. With processor running, slowly drizzle in the olive oil to produce a thin emulsion. Place sauce in a bowl, cover, and leave at room temperature until ready to use. Yield: about 1 cup.

Tropical Pineapple-Mango Relish

1 cup medium-diced fresh pineapple
1 cup diced and peeled seedless cucumber
1/2 cup medium-diced fresh mango
1/3 cup chopped red onion
1 teaspoon finely diced fresh jalapeño pepper
1 tablespoon chopped fresh cilantro
1/4 cup freshly squeezed lime juice (about 1 1/2 limes)

Combine all ingredients in a medium bowl and cover tightly. If not using within 1 hour, refrigerate until ready to use. Yield: about 2 1/4 cups.

Assembly

2 (7-inch) pieces smoked Polish sausage (kielbasa)
12 ounces beer (do not use light beer)
2 hoagie- or Portuguese-style rolls
Lemon Garlic Sauce
Tropical Pineapple-Mango Relish

Place sausage in a medium frying pan and add beer. Cook sausage over medium heat for 20 minutes. Preheat grill or broiler. Remove sausage from beer, slice each sausage almost in half, and brown on grill or in broiler, about 5 minutes. Meanwhile, generously brush the inside of the rolls with the Lemon Garlic Sauce. Place rolls under the broiler until golden. Place a sausage in each roll, spoon on the Tropical Pineapple-Mango Relish to taste, and serve immediately. Serves 2.

Hawaii's Favorite Hot Dog Condiments

Mustard lovers take note—Aunty Lilikoi produces all manner of passion fruit products, including passion fruit mustard (offered as an optional condiment at Puka Dog) and passion fruit wasabi mustard. For ordering information, contact: Aunty Lilikoi, 9633 Kaumuali'i Highway, Waimea, Kaua'i, Hawaii, (866) LILIKOI, www.auntylilikoi.com. Hawaiians also adore soy sauce, which they call shoyu, on just about everything, including hot dogs. Hawaiin shoyu has a sweet-salty taste in comparison to traditional soy sauces that are known for their sharp, somewhat bitter, flavor. The major manufacturer of Hawaiian shoyu is Aloha Shoyu Company on the island of O'ahu. For information on purchasing shoyu, contact: Aloha Shoyu Company, 96-1205 Waihona Street, Pearl City, HI 96782, (808) 456-5929, www.alohashoyu.com.

Oregon

Good Dog Bad Dog

708 SW Alder Street, Portland, OR 97205

(503) 222-3410

Good Dog Bad Dog is definitely not your average hot dog eatery. It's what many in Portland call a sausage shop, and the appellation is well deserved. Owner Ted Gamble established the business in 1981, and he makes all the sausages in-house, which accounts for why the place is closed on Saturdays, dedicated to sausage making. Grilled choices include the Oregon Smokey made with molasses, smoked over hickory, and served with grilled onions and horseradish; the mild British

Banger perked up with a horseradish sauce; sweet Italian sausage served with grilled onions, mozzarella cheese, and marinara sauce; and a nicely spiced bratwurst. A favorite topping is fried onions that can be ordered with a healthy dose of fresh garlic. Sides are reminiscent of picnic fare, including potato salad and baked beans.

Oregon Brats with Garlic Onions

Ted Gamble's popular onion and garlic topping is delicious with all kinds of sausages and hot dogs.

Grilled Onions with Garlic

1 tablespoon vegetable oil
2 large onions, thinly sliced
1 tablespoon butter
2 large cloves garlic, finely chopped

In a medium frying pan, heat the oil, add the onions and slowly sauté over medium-low heat until soft, about 20 minutes. Add the butter and sauté 10 minutes more, or until onions are well browned. Add the garlic the last minute of cooking.

Assembly

2 bratwurst, grilled
2 crusty French-style rolls, toasted
Grilled Onions with Garlic
Horseradish (optional)
Brown German-style mustard (optional)

Place grilled bratwurst in the toasted rolls, top with the Grilled Onions with Garlic and add horseradish and/or mustard if desired. Serves 2.

Washington

Cyber-Dogs

909 Pike Street, Seattle, WA

(206) 405-DOGS

www.cyber-dogs.com

Seattle, Washington, is said to be one of the healthiest cities in America, and residents, including die-hard carnivores, are devoted to the many vegetarian options, including hot dogs, that abound in the land of green cuisine. Cyber-Dogs is located in Seattle's downtown Capitol Hill neighborhood at the Convention Center. Tania Harrison established her Internet café in 2002. The ever-so-small vegetarian dog house, characterized by its bright orange walls, specializes in internationally-themed tofu hot dogs. The standard menu includes the Indian "DoggiLama" that comes with choices like masala, spinach sauce, cucumber yogurt sauce, and fresh greens; the "Greek Goddess" with a choice of hummus, vinaigrette, feta cheese, and pepperoncini; and the Italian "Dogalisa" with a choice of marinara sauce, pesto sauce, Parmesan cheese, and fresh greens. Diners can choose to have their dogs on a panino roll or a whole-grain roll from Essential Baking Company in Seattle.

Vegetarian Pesto Dog

Pesto

2 cups fresh basil leaves, washed and dried

1 teaspoon kosher salt

1 teaspoon freshly ground pepper

2 large cloves garlic, finely chopped

1/2 cup quality extra virgin olive oil

1/4 cup pine (pignola) nuts

1/4 cup freshly grated Parmesan cheese

1/4 cup freshly grated Romano cheese

Place all ingredients except cheese into a food processor and blend until smooth. Transfer to a bowl, and stir in the cheese. Refrigerate, covered, for 2 hours to allow flavors to blend. Yield: 1 1/2 cups.

Assembly

1 soy hot dog, boiled in beer for 1 minute

1 whole-grain roll

2 tablespoons Pesto, or to taste

Fresh mixed greens

Place the soy dog on the roll, top with Pesto and mixed greens, and serve immediately. Serves 1.

Soy and Tofu "Not Dogs"

According to the *Soy Daily* at www.thesoydailyclub.com, soy hot dogs are precooked and require care in preparation to avoid overcooking. Recommended methods are pan frying in a small amount of butter for 1 to 2 minutes; microwaving for 30 seconds; and boiling in water or beer for 1 to 2 minutes. Popular brands of "not dogs" include Soyboy from Northern Soy, Inc. (www.soyboy.com); Tofu Pups from Lightlife (www.lightlife.com); and Yves Tofu and Veggie Dogs from Yves Veggie Cuisine (www.yvesveggie.com).

More Cool Dogs in Seattle

Diggity Dog Hot Dog and Sausage Company

5421 Meridian Avenue North, Seattle, WA 98103

(206) 633-1966

Matt's Famous Chili Dogs

6615 E. Marginal Way South, Seattle, WA 98108

(206) 768-0418

www.mattsfamouschilidogs.com

The Frankfurter

Seattle Center

305 Harrison Street, Seattle, WA 98104

(206) 728-7243

www.thefrankfurter.com

Uli's Famous Sausage, L.L.C.

1511 Pike Place Market, Seattle, WA 98101

(206) 839-1000

www.ulisfamoussausage.com

Index

143

Metric Conversion Chart

Liquid and Dry Measures

U.S.	Canadian	Australian
¼ teaspoon	1 mL	1 ml
½ teaspoon	2 mL	2 ml
1 teaspoon	5 mL	5 ml
1 Tablespoon	15 mL	20 ml
¼ cup	50 mL	60 ml
⅓ cup	75 mL	80 ml
½ cup	125 mL	125 ml
⅔ cup	150 mL	170 ml
¾ cup	175 mL	190 ml
1 cup	250 mL	250 ml
1 quart	1 liter	1 litre

Temperature Conversion Chart

Fahrenheit	Celsius
250	120
275	140
300	150
325	160
350	180
375	190
400	200
425	220
450	230
475	240
500	260